The Exorcism Files

Also by Adam Blai:

The Catholic Guide to Miracles:
Separating the Authentic from the Counterfeit

Adam Blai

THE
Exorcism
FILES

True Stories of
Demonic Possession

SOPHIA INSTITUTE PRESS
Manchester, New Hampshire

Sophia Institute Press
Box 5284, Manchester, NH 03108
1-800-888-9344
www.SophiaInstitute.com

Sophia Institute Press is a registered trademark of Sophia Institute.

paperback ISBN 978-1-64413-508-2

ebook ISBN 978-1-64413-509-9

Library of Congress Control Number: 2022938954

First printing

For my father, who was supportive and encouraged me to keep going

Contents

Part I
Introduction to Another World

Part II
Learning the Ropes

Appendices

Preface

It is human nature all the way back to Adam and Eve: we do not like to be told what to do. More than that, we are suspicious of anyone who says they know better than we do. When other people struggle at going it alone, we assume it is their problem (and probably their own fault). We think we will not make the same mistakes or we are simply stronger than they. So into the world we go, making our own choices, each of us reinventing the wheel. Of course, there are many who take advantage of this tendency toward willfulness and suspicion in order to shape our ideas and our views and to exploit our naivete for their own profit. Eventually, hopefully, life trades youth for wisdom, and we start to see the value in the rules of morality and propriety our forebearers tried to pass down to us.

We can see this part of our fallen nature playing out in the secularization of our civilization. The warnings—against sin and falsehoods and especially the dark supernatural powers that exist in our world—that used to be baked into society are no longer passed down, and they are no longer reflected in our stories and traditions. Even the clergy these days are rarely trained in the reality of the spiritual world. Many Catholics, lay and clergy, are simply embarrassed to openly take the spiritual seriously.

We have wandered away from our spiritual traditions and forgotten the lessons from millennia of experience. Though we may have left behind the supernatural, it has not left us behind. Religion used to provide answers and rituals to help us understand the things we cannot understand with only our wits and our senses. Now, increasingly, we search for answers in ways previous generations knew to be dangerous, and so we play with spiritual forces we do not understand and cannot control.

This book is not about telling you what to do, or not to do—at least in the sense of a collection of rules. We know that does not cut it in today's world. Instead, this book is about telling stories—real stories, *my* stories—about the reality of the spiritual world and the dark forces that move about in that world and influence this one. These stories may not prove the old warnings and lessons about the spiritual world in a strictly scientific way, but my hope is that they will demonstrate the wisdom of the past and make the intangible feel, maybe for the first time, real.

Now, what about the harm that could be done in relaying true stories about the dark powers? This is a concern that has given me pause over the years. I absolutely do not want to encourage people to interact with these spiritual creatures, but only and always to seek God. I do not want to inspire amateur dabblers who think they are competent to confront or control fallen angels. These stories clearly illustrate that these creatures are evil and purely destructive. Without fail, those who have been freed from their grasp wish to warn the world about what got them into trouble—and to never, ever try to contact or converse with them again.

I have also been very careful not to include any identifying information in these accounts. Therefore, in most cases, I have changed details such as names, places, and dates so that the stories are complete but do not expose particular people. (The exceptions are cases I worked on that have been discussed publicly elsewhere.) Where it made narrative sense, I have also combined multiple stories into one.

One last note: you might suppose that the stories included here are unusual or extraordinary in some way. It is true that I tried to pick interesting ones, but, the fact is, these stories are representative of many, many more cases that will never be published.

The Exorcism Files

Introduction

Before we jump into these stories, some basic background information may be helpful.

The focus of this book is the troublesome, deceptive spirits that humankind has dealt with from the very beginning. In Christianity, they are called fallen angels or demons; in Islam they are called *djinn* or *shaitan*; in Judaism they are called *dybbuk*; in some branches of Buddhism, they are called animal spirits; and in Native American religions, they have various names depending on the tribe. Further, there is some version of an exorcist in all these traditions: people who have the knowledge and power to drive away these spirits from the people whom they are troubling. These cases are usually rare, and this driving away usually takes the form of a religious ceremony or rite that is considered a difficult and somewhat dangerous thing to do.

These stories come from the Roman Catholic tradition, though they touch on other traditions in a few cases. The Catholic Church has been doing exorcisms since her establishment by Jesus Christ, who gave explicit instructions to His Church to cast out demons. Seven of the major miracles recounted in the Gospels are exorcisms, and exorcism was already well known to the Jewish people in the time of Jesus: there were Jewish exorcists operating in society before and during His time. Over the centuries, the Church developed and then standardized the exorcism rite—a fixed ritual with a precise text and instructions to take certain actions. She also gradually restricted who could do exorcisms, and when. Today, we have an old exorcism rite from 1614 and a revised one from 1999.

The old rite first has the solemn exorcism, which can only be used for a possessed person. This rite can only be done by a priest with permission from their bishop. If someone else attempts to use it, he will have no authority over the fallen angels, and the experience will likely end very badly for that person. The rite is quite long; solemn exorcisms generally last between one and three hours, or even longer, per session. It is a Hollywood myth that exorcisms are over in one dramatic prayer session: they can take from one session to years of weekly sessions, depending on the person and how many demons have taken up residence in them. The bishop, meanwhile, only gives permission to use the solemn exorcism after there is enough evidence to have moral certainty that the person truly is possessed.

There are four classic signs of possession that can give us that certainty. These were developed over many centuries of experience by a Church that was skeptical and trying to debunk claims of possession—not because Church leaders did not believe in the demonic, but because they knew, even centuries ago, that there were often other explanations for the claims of the "possessed." And to perform a solemn exorcism on someone who does not need it, besides being a waste of time, can confirm the person in their delusion, or other conditions, and distract from the help they really need.

The four signs of possession are: understanding and speaking all languages, knowing secret details the person could not know by natural means, reacting against the holy (objects, persons, and so on), and strength beyond their physical condition. First, fallen angels know all languages, a sign that cannot be produced by epilepsy or mental illness. We have many instances of the possessed person being questioned in languages they did not know and either responding correctly in English or in that language. We also have many instances of the possessed person speaking or writing in languages they do not know. Second, the possessed person often mentions or recounts the details of the lives of people present. This is usually the priests, but if they think they can drive away others they will try. They also seem to enjoy mocking people who do not believe in them by recounting their secret sins. Third, the possessed can tell what is blessed and what is not. They will refuse to touch or drink a water bottle that has been secretly blessed and be fine with others that have not; they can name the saint's relic you have in your pocket; and they will avoid the chair that has a few grains of blessed salt lost in the carpet under it. Fourth and finally, people can have an amazing strength when possessed. This does not happen in each case, but when it does, it is clearly not human. A mother might lift a car off her child in a single burst of adrenaline, but the possessed keep it up for hours, long past when a normal body would collapse.

The old rite also has what is often called a "minor exorcism." This is an expansion on the original prayer to St. Michael, written by Pope Leo XIII. That original prayer is much longer than the St. Michael prayer said so often today and can be said only by priests. The original intent was to combat Freemasonry, which was attempting to destroy the Church in the late nineteenth century. This minor exorcism is usually used for houses or land, as well as particular objects that may be cursed, which is simply the opposite of blessed, with the object having been given over in some way to the demonic. Exorcising a house is usually completed in one or two visits, much faster than a person. The minor exorcism is also sometimes used as a diagnostic for possession, as it usually causes demons to manifest in a possessed person so the signs of possession can be evaluated.

The Church also intervenes for souls in Purgatory that signal their need for prayer, often called a haunting. These "poor souls," as they are called, are those who passed their judgment to go to Heaven but still have imperfections left over from the sins in their life. These imperfections are resolved in Purgatory, which takes time. We can speed up that process by offering prayers and Masses for them. Unlike demons, poor souls do not talk with the living or respond to spirit communication, such as ghost hunters or Ouija boards. It is a serious sin to call up the dead to talk with them, which is called *necromancy* in Scripture. The most common places where we see poor-soul activity are churches, rectories, monasteries, and places where murders or suicides happened. Poor souls are usually helped in one visit by prayers for them, and they do not recur after that.

Spiritually, exorcisms are the work of the entire Church, but in the physical world they are performed by real individuals. In fact, those of us involved in exorcism ministry on a regular basis become well known to the demonic and seemingly hated more by them. And it goes the other way, too: we meet the same fallen angels over and over in different cases over the years. Sometimes, as in my case, Satan becomes directly involved in trying to tempt and destroy a person who is involved in opposing his kingdom on earth. This is not a concern for the person seeking to serve God as well as possible, as God is the Creator. Satan is merely a creature, and God is in control of him as with all other creatures.

Hollywood would have us believe that Satan is an independent operator, even a charming and misunderstood figure, vastly powerful and free to do whatever he wants. The truth is far from that. Satan is a fallen angel who was created at the beginning of time with the other angels, then banished from Heaven for his disobedience. He chose to be permanently cut off from God. Now he is relegated to serving God in spite of himself, tempting mankind and thereby providing the spiritual struggles that lead to spiritual strengthening.

He is just a fallen angel, not a god, and certainly not even a millionth as powerful as the Creator of the universe. As a mere creature, like us, he relies on the will of God to remain in existence at each moment and on the permissive will of God to take any action. We see this clearly spelled out in the Book of Job and in the interactions of the demons with Jesus: in the exorcism of the Gerasene demoniac in the Gospel of Mark (5:1–20), they even must ask permission to go into the pigs. What a sad state compared to the Heaven they gave up! But, give it up they did: they do not want pity, and they do not want to repent. They only want to tempt, to oppress, and to possess as many people as possible in order to stop them from making it back to God.

Part I

Introduction to Another World

In which I discover the reality of the demonic through the fakeness of reality TV and see things I never expected

Chapter 1

Modern Spiritualism and the
Paranormal TV Craze

Spiritualism—the act of seeking communication with the spirits of the dead, known in Scripture as *necromancy*—has always been with humankind. It can take the form of asking the dead to make some manifestation, like to make a noise, to appear as a ghost, or to speak to or through a living person (often called a *medium* or, in ancient times, *sorcerer*). Sometimes the interaction is more indirect, such as interpreting random events thought to be influenced by spirits to divine the future.

Most cultures see spiritualism as a form of magic that can only be performed by people with secret knowledge, or who possess spiritual "gifts" of some kind, or both. In many cultures, spiritualism, and magic in general, is distrusted, and the people who practice it are pushed to the margins of society. For Jews and Christians, spiritualism is strongly forbidden altogether: appealing to any spirit other than God is an appeal to a mere creature and an insult to the Creator. We see this reflected in a number of Old Testament verses.

First, we have two verses warning the Jews not to adopt the spiritual practices of the people living in the Promised Land and which address how God feels about turning to created spirits for guidance:

When you come into the land which the LORD, your God, is giving you, you shall not learn to imitate the abominations of the nations there. Let there not be found among you anyone who causes their son or daughter to pass through the fire, or practices divination, or is a soothsayer, augur, or sorcerer, or who casts spells, consults ghosts and spirits, or seeks oracles from the dead. Anyone who does such things is an abomination to the Lord, and because of such abominations the LORD, your God, is dispossessing them before you. You must be altogether sincere with the LORD, your God. Although these nations whom you are about to dispossess listen to their soothsayers and diviners, the LORD, your God, will not permit you to do so. A prophet like me will the LORD, your God, raise up for you from among your own kindred; that is the one to whom you shall listen. (Deut. 18:9–15)

Should anyone turn to ghosts and spirits and prostitute oneself with them, I will turn against that person and cut such a one off from among the people. (Lev. 20:6)

The word *abomination* means a thing that causes disgust and hatred. We also learn that God will withdraw His gifts from the person who engages in conjuring the spirits of the dead, thereby dispossessing them. Here are two more warnings—one that warns that such acts defile us and one that warns of the consequences:

Do not turn to ghosts or consult spirits, by which you will be defiled. I, the LORD, am your God. (Lev. 19:31)

And when they say to you, "Inquire of ghosts and soothsayers who chirp and mutter; should not a people inquire of their gods, consulting the dead on behalf of the living, for instruction and testimony?" Surely, those who speak like this are the ones for whom there is no dawn. He will pass through it hard-pressed and hungry, and when hungry, shall become enraged, and curse king and gods. He will look upward, and will gaze at the earth, but will see only distress and darkness, oppressive gloom, murky, without light. (Isa. 8:19–22)

The person ends up deprived of the good things in life, as well as hungry and angry. They curse the "gods" they have chosen to follow and see the world through a pall of depression and gloom.

The first of the Ten Commandments, which are themselves a summary of the 613 Judaic laws, reinforces the importance of not turning to spirits other than God. Here it is given in Exodus:

I am the LORD your God, who brought you out of the land of Egypt, out of the house of slavery. You shall not have other gods beside me. (Exod. 20:2–3)

and when Jesus is asked what the most important commandment is, He responds,

He said to him, "You shall love the Lord, your God, with all your heart, with all your soul, and with all your mind. This is the greatest and the first commandment." (Matt. 22:37–38)

So, we see that the Old Testament prohibition against seeking communication with ghosts and spirits is strong, and Jesus affirms this by stating that the most important commandment is to love God alone. To seek information, consolation, or power from a spirit other than God is to treat that spirit like a god and to cease to fully trust and love the true God completely.

Nevertheless, the Jews of the Old Testament did go on to adopt some of the gods, beliefs, and spiritual practices of the Canaanites. For them, and for modern people, the lure of information, power, and consolation was powerful. It is apparently easy to forget God's warning against these spirits — that what they provide is a sham that eventually leads to deprivation, anger, distress, and spiritual darkness.

Fast-forward to the nineteenth century: in 1848 the Fox sisters, eleven-year-old Kate and fourteen-year-old Maggie, were living in Hydesville, New York. They started scamming their parents in the following way, related by Maggie forty years later, after their careers as "mediums" had ended:

> When we went to bed at night we used to tie an apple to a string and move the string up and down, causing the apple to bump on the floor, or we would drop the apple on the floor, making a strange noise every time it would rebound. Mother listened to this for a time. She would not understand it and did not suspect us as being capable of a trick because we were so young.[1]

By pulling the string, the girls could make the "spirits" that haunted the house answer questions: one thud for no, two for yes, and so on. Well, word started to spread. It is important to understand that there was no common idea of mediums, psychics, or the paranormal at the time. There certainly have always been ghost stories and attempts to conjure the dead, as we said, but a spirit performing *on demand* like this was new. As their act developed, the "spirit" claimed to be a man who had been murdered in the

---

[1] Harry Houdini, *A Magician among the Spirits* (Cambridge: Cambridge University Press, 2011), 1–17.

house. The townsfolk searched for someone who had lived in the house previously. Maggie related later:

> Finally, they found a man by the name of Bell, and they said that this poor innocent man had committed a murder in the house and that the noises had come from the spirit of the murdered person. Poor Bell was shunned and looked upon by the whole community as a murderer.[2]

By their simple deception, the Fox sisters started the first modern wave of spiritualism in the western world. They triggered the emergence of an entire industry of charlatans who claimed to have on-demand contact with the dead, almost always for a fee. In a time before television, it became popular to hire a medium to communicate with your dead loved ones or for people to mimic their methods at home themselves. In addition to the common people's interest in spiritualism, the wealthy got involved. The Society for Psychical Research (SPR) was founded in 1882 in London to research spiritualism and related phenomena such as extra sensory perception from a more scientific perspective. (Prominent members included, ironically enough, *Sherlock Holmes* author Sir Arthur Conan Doyle.) In spite of this, a lot of their work consisted of accepting and cataloging ghost stories from the public. Some magicians of the day, particularly Harry Houdini, made it their mission to discredit and debunk spiritualism and everything related.[3]

---

[2] Houdini, *A Magician among the Spirits*, 17.
[3] This skeptical magician tradition has continued to this day in the form of the James Randi Educational Foundation (JREF). James Randi is a magician and had a standing offer of a million dollars to anyone who could produce paranormal phenomenon under laboratory conditions. The money was there for decades, and nobody ever took it.

Meanwhile, two years after Maggie's confession in 1890 that the Fox sisters' thudding house spirit was a hoax, Elijah Bond submitted his patent for the board and planchette that would be known as the Ouija board. This made spiritualism even more accessible for the average family. At the same time, the mysterious, the eastern, and the occult were in vogue. Egyptology became all the rage in Europe, and even satanic themed organizations like "The Hellfire Club" gained notoriety.

Then World War I came, leaving countless families bereft and longing for their lost loved ones. This caused a surge of interest in communicating with the dead. Margaret Murray was an amateur anthropologist who had an interest in ancient religions. During the war, she developed her "witch-cult hypothesis," which held that Christianity had stamped out an older pagan religion devoted to a horned god. In her theoretical religion, the women were led by one man who played the role of the horned god, and each year he was killed and replaced by a new man. Her theory proposed that the women performed various kinds of magic and recounted their activity to the man once a year. This theory gained attention, even leading to an article in the *Encyclopedia Britannica*, the ultimate authority at the time. Her article ran for forty years, until her theory was discredited. But by the time the *Encyclopedia* wrote a retraction, it was too late: the modern idea of witches had been established in the culture.

One of the people who bought into her theory was Gerald Gardner, the father of modern witchcraft. (He called his system "witchcraft" and the people who practiced it "Wiccans.") He thought he found a group of people practicing Margaret's ancient religion in 1930s England, and so he combined their ideas with what he learned from other occult groups, creating his own religion. In 1954, he wrote *Witchcraft Today*, which got some attention, but he remained obscure. It was when he appeared on the BBC that the world learned that there were real people claiming to be witches. Largely due to him, there was a wave of interest in witchcraft, Satanism, and the occult in the 1960s, particularly in cinema. Today, despite being concocted less than a century ago and being based on a bogus theory, Wicca is widely recognized as a legitimate religion, and it still claims to have ancient roots.

After the 1970s, there was a lull in mainstream interest in the occult. The reasons are hard to pin down: perhaps it was the prosperity, security, and materialism of the 80s and 90s, combined with mounting confidence in strictly scientific explanations for everything. But this lull did not last, and soon television ushered in a new era of interest in spiritualism.

It is hard to imagine a time when there were no television shows chronicling the paranormal, but it all started in 2004 with *Ghost Hunters*. At the time, I was in graduate school for adult clinical psychology at Penn State and working in a brainwave research lab. It was not at all mainstream to be involved in spiritualism, and the idea of ghost-hunting was off most people's radar. There were those who were interested, of course, but spiritualism was very much a niche topic. The TV show *Ghost Hunters* featured two normal people trying to investigate sites of hauntings with modern technology. Gone was the Ouija board and the medium, replaced by the digital recorder and night-vision cameras. Within a few years, there were a few more ghost-hunting shows, and soon they were all over cable television. The next wave of spiritualism had started.

I had been trained in diagnosis of mental illness and had treated a number of cases in our training clinic. I had also seen research on hypnosis that demonstrated that the otherwise healthy brain can produce hallucinations on command if a person is especially susceptible to hypnosis. When I noticed the paranormal TV shows,

I did some research into the psychological literature, curious as to whether this alleged paranormal activity was just a hallucination, mild mental illness, scam, or perhaps something spiritual. I became the staff advisor to a paranormal research group at Penn State, and I learned some of the history of ghost hunting and the ideas around it. Soon I was able to go visit a few cases where people complained of strange events in their houses. It ended up leading me on the surprising path to exorcisms that has defined my life.

Chapter 2

A Clueless Encounter

Hypnosis is one of the last real mysteries of psychology and brain science. We still do not know exactly what it is or how it works. The ability to be hypnotized does not seem to serve any useful function. In fact, hypnosis seems only to make people vulnerable to the influence of others and certainly less aware of their environ- ment while they are entranced. The popular and reassuring myths about hypnosis—that you cannot be hypnotized against your will or that you cannot be made to do harm to yourself or others—are just not true.

The brainwave lab I worked in during graduate school had been studying hypnosis for many years, and so I read much of the scientific literature on it. In the 1960s, there were many studies that today would be (rightly) considered unethical. These studies included hypnotizing people to reach into a box with a rattlesnake (de-fanged, but they did not know that), to reach into what they thought was a bowl of acid, and to pick up a revolver and attempt to shoot some- one (it was not a functioning gun and was unloaded). Modern stage hypnotists downplay the potential power of hypnosis and claim it is harmless. They usually perform what is more akin to a group power-of-suggestion exercise rather than a deep hypnotic trance.

What seems to be true is that you either are hypnotizable, or you are not. Most people are somewhat hypnotizable; some are completely unresponsive to hypnosis; and some fall deeply into a trance and can be made to hallucinate on command. It is a trait that is consistent across one's lifespan: if you test as highly hypnotizable in adolescence, you will still do so when you are sixty. On the other hand, if you can't be hypnotized, there is no way to learn how to be. You can learn to respond to suggestions, but a real hypnotic trance that can produce strong false experiences is different.

I learned group and individual hypnosis for our lab studies; I did my masters on changes in brain organization during shifts in consciousness while experiencing a hypnotic trance; and I used hypnosis in a few clinical settings when it seemed indicated. I was not a big fan of hypnosis clinically, as I thought it was usually better to work with the conscious mind than the unconscious. I did see that hypnosis, if used very carefully, can be used to recover memories of events the conscious mind had forgotten. There is, however, a great danger of using leading questions and subtle suggestions to cause the mind to manufacture false memories of events that never happened. This is because the entranced person's mind is responsive to any suggestion and will attempt to comply with them. That is what led to most of the false memory cases that caused the satanic panic in the 1990s.

The second haunted house case I participated in was about two hours from Penn State, where a couple was renting an older house in a rougher part of town. They had lived there for several years and had experienced problems for most of that time. They saw black, smoky forms moving through the house, heard inexplicable loud bangs, had objects go missing only to return days later in very odd locations in the house, and even experienced the sensation of being grabbed and thrown down the stairs by seemingly nothing. The local newspaper had come and written about the haunting for the paper, including a photo of what looked like a ball of solid black smoke, a little smaller than a basketball. This had appeared the instant a loud bang occurred, which scared the reporters so badly they took that one picture and left.

I arrived at the house earlier than everyone else on a hot summer day. The couple took me on a tour to point out where various events happened and to show me photos they took with their phones. Phones with cameras were a new thing at that time, and I came across a number of photos of the same black forms that appeared in earlier cases. Then it seems that the spirits got wise to the cameras, and these images were no longer captured.

The house was not air-conditioned, so the windows were open for ventilation. We were upstairs and had just stepped into the bedroom when there was a bang like a .22 pistol being fired in the bathroom. It startled everyone and cut off our conversation. But they seemed less concerned than I was, explaining that such noises were normal in the house. I immediately checked the bathroom for any sign of broken glass, a broken tile, or anything that could account for the sound. Nothing was out of place or damaged. Things were quiet for the rest of the tour; they said it often went quiet for a while after acting up like that.

The boyfriend was a stocky, tough-looking man. He told me that he had been drunk one weekend and yelled out to whatever was harassing them. He called it a coward for attacking his girlfriend and challenged it to fight him. Nothing happened right away. But later that night, he awoke in bed to see a black form floating over him. He immediately felt large hands clamp around his neck, which he said felt like iron. He was repeatedly slammed against the mattress while being choked, and then it was gone. They took photos of the bruises on his neck, which they showed to me. He had slept on the couch in the living room since that encounter. It seemed to me that this was a tactic to separate the two and eventually to drive him to move out. Whatever was happening in the house was more focused on the woman.

The first night, I spent the time interviewing the couple about various details and experiences. I also informally evaluated them for signs of mental illness. The second night, the woman made a particular request of me. She explained that she had a recurring experience while drifting off to sleep. She slept on a mattress on the floor and would suddenly find herself half asleep and unable to move. The form of a person pulling themselves along the floor with their hands would approach her. It would come up and whisper in her ear for a long time, but she could never quite remember what it had said. She asked me to hypnotize her in an attempt to recover her memory of its words.

I was hesitant to use hypnosis in this situation, and so I talked with a few people with more experience than I had. In the end, I agreed to try a brief and shallow hypnotic session to see if we could recover her memories. She lay down on the bed and I sat on a nearby chair, and with her consent, the whole session was video recorded for documentation. After some instructions and explanations, I started a standard hypnotic induction like we had used in group hypnosis with students for many years.

I got about halfway through the induction, and then something very strange happened. A raspy male voice snidely said, "What do you think you're doing? We are in charge here, she is ours. Get out of here!"

I tried to speak to the woman, addressing her by name. She did not respond, and the male voice started laughing. I then tried to bring her out of the hypnotic trance in the usual way, but nothing happened. The voice continued, "You don't know what you are doing. We are going to have fun with you tonight."

For the next two hours, the voices alternated between what sounded like the woman, a raspy male voice, and other voices that sounded different still. The woman's voice would describe being terrified, saying that she was watching the scene play out from outside of her body; she could see herself laying there and me sitting in the chair. Then the other voices would mock me some more. I was trying to think psychologically about this—whether it was a psychotic experience brought on by the start of a trance, or whether some Post-Traumatic Stress Disorder response had been triggered. At the same time, it very much felt like I was in a horror movie: she looked and sounded like someone who was possessed.

All the psychological techniques I could think of had no impact. Simultaneously, the woman was not moving an inch, lying perfectly still in bed. If this was a psychotic reaction, I would expect the person to move, to run away, or even to attack me. In addition, there was a palpable feeling in the room, a kind of electrical charge in the air and the sense of a threatening presence. After about an hour and a half, I started to pray. I mostly said the Our Father and the Hail Mary. I also asked God for help, since I had no idea what else to do. The first voice spoke up, "You want us to let you talk with her again? We will leave at 2:30 a.m. for thirty minutes, you can talk with her then. Then we will be back."

I continued to pray, and at two thirty in the morning, the woman suddenly came back to her senses and sat up. She said she had been conscious the whole time but was watching from what seemed like twenty feet away. The woman saw herself talking but had no control of her body or her voice. She was very shaken and upset, though not hysterical. She also was very lucid; she was not acting psychotic. The woman went to the kitchen to get water, and we all continued to talk. I then took ten minutes to step outside and call my father. I was shaken by the experience and felt a deep certainty that those voices were spirits—demons—and not a mental disorder. It helped to talk with my father, who asked sobering questions and was open to all the possibilities.

At about three, she said she needed to lie down for a minute since she had a headache. As she lay down, she became completely slack and unconscious. A nasty smile crept across her face, and that voice said, "We said we would be back. You still don't know what you are doing."

I do not remember many details about the last hour or so of that night. I know I prayed a lot more, and eventually she came back to her senses and went to sleep. I wasn't sure what I had seen or how to make sense of it. It certainly looked nothing like any hypnosis session I had experienced or imagined, and it did not fit with the types of mental illness that can cause strange voices or psychotic experiences. There was also that electric feeling in the room and that sense of presence I had never experienced before.

I learned by experience that night that possession may, in fact, be real. This was a world-changing event for me, and the implications were huge. If possession was real, then demons were real. That means that God and the devil are concrete realities and not vague notions we just say we believe in. That means that we are accountable to God for our choices and that there is an enemy moving through the world trying to destroy us. If all of that were true, then I had to reorient my life based on that reality. Ghost hunting was no longer an interesting hobby; there was a real spiritual war going on. It took weeks of reflection, but that case was the turning point for me, and it started my journey toward where I am today.

Chapter 3

Wicca, Witchcraft, and Fables, Oh My!

While Wicca is now recognized as a legitimate religion, it does not really have any centralized structure or beliefs. There are innumerable systems of thought and practice that call themselves Wicca or witchcraft, and there is no unifying theology or set of religious traditions or texts. Some worship the earth; some worship a goddess; some focus only on household magic; and some even explicitly worship Satan. As we have discussed, there are also many different origin stories about Wicca, depending on which source you use.

Like other New Age systems, Wicca uses some basic tricks to attract people: the feeling that you are uniquely special, the idea that you have magical powers, and the sense that you are at the center of religion instead of God. This is achieved by convincing you that you have tapped into some hidden tradition known only to a special elect and that your imagined powers are a sign of your giftedness above others. The illusion of magical powers gives you a sense of control in life—over future events and even people in your life. This is particularly powerful for people who have been harmed and feel that life itself is threatening. By putting yourself at the center of your religious beliefs, there is also no external standard to be judged by. This is attractive because we all like to rationalize and judge ourselves to be a "good person." Nobody wants to be held to objective standards that may show we aren't who we think we are.

So, one consistent trait of Wiccan beliefs is a self-centered philosophy with illusions of power over life. In some cases, accepting this belief seems to have actual effects. Sometimes it may be coincidence, like fortune cookie "wisdom" that is true for most people but seems to apply directly to us. In other cases, actual demonic spirits may respond to the request for their assistance through black magic and will usually feed the delusions described above. They may pretend to serve the practitioner of whatever magic system they are using, feigning deference to the "powerful witch" or "powerful wizard." In reality, demonic spirits could not care less about the rituals or words people use; you gain no power over fallen angels by wiggling your fingers or muttering words. But the demons will play along with the person for a long time if he or she is bringing others into the same trap, or they may turn on the person who tries to leave the relationship. If the person is serving the demons by promoting them, they may wait until the person is older and close to dying and thus no longer useful. This is a type of case exorcists see.

Before we discuss a case study of someone who tried to turn away from the witchcraft trap, we should clarify what witchcraft really is and how it relates to Wicca.

There are mentions of black magic of various kinds in the Bible: necromancy (calling upon spirits of the dead to communicate with them, or ghost hunting), divination of the future (only God actually knows the future, but demons sometimes predict things and then make them happen to fool us), trying to conjure secret knowledge about people, human sacrifice to demonic spirits (such as the infant sacrifices to Canaanite gods), and other rarer displays such as the manifestations performed by the Pharoah's magicians to refute the God of Moses. The Bible strongly forbids black magic because, like the New Age, it violates the First Commandment by putting other spirits (or other persons, including the self) before God.

The idea of black magic is an ancient idea, but Wicca is not. Modern Wicca started, as we said in the introduction, with Margaret Alice Murray (1863–1963). She was interested in many topics: Egyptology, archaeology, anthropology, and folklore. She was very accomplished in these areas and was an effective activist for women's rights. During WWI, she, like most people in England, could not travel for quite some time. It was then that she developed her witch-cult hypothesis, based on her reading of documents from earlier witch trials—much earlier than the popularized Salem witch trials in America. She imagined an ancient, pre-Christian religion that was practiced by these witches.

The cult, she hypothesized, had a number of traits that will sound familiar to many:

- It was organized into covens of thirteen members, twelve women and one man.
- The coven worshiped a horned male god.
- The records of the coven were kept in a secret book.
- Meetings were either called Sabbaths for religious ceremonies or Esbats for business meetings.
- Four types of sacrifice were used: writing one's name in blood to join, killing animals, killing children, and the burning of the group's male figure at the end of the year.

Her theory was published in a book, *The Witch-Cult in Western Europe*, in 1921. The book did not sell very well, but it caused her to be regarded by some as an authority on witchcraft, in part due to her credibility from her mainstream academic work in archaeology and anthropology. In 1929, the *Encyclopedia Britannica* invited her to write the entry on witchcraft. She submitted her theory and presented it as if it were universally accepted, while, in reality, it was heavily criticized by scholars for lacking any real evidence.

In 1931, likely prompted by the new attention given to her theory, Murray published a more successful book in a popular style called *The God of the Witches*. She introduced the phrase "the Old Religion" to describe her proposed cult. She also removed many of the traits that made the cult seem evil to the average person: the sacrifice of children and animals, as well as group sex. Murray increased the mystique of this cult by saying it went back to Paleolithic times (over ten thousand years ago). She also expanded the territory of the cult from England to all of Europe, Asia, and part of Africa.

Two decades later, she wrote a third book, taking her theory even further. She claimed that societies all over the world made blood sacrifices of their kings to nature gods. This last book was mostly ignored, even by her supporters.

Remember that in 1929 there was no internet, and many people did not have easy access to libraries. Many families, however, did have access to an encyclopedia. It was the Wikipedia of its day, having articles on just about every conceivable topic. If it was in the encyclopedia, it could be trusted and cited as fact. So, when the *Encyclopedia Britannica* ran Murray's article from 1929 until 1969, her theory, though completely baseless, became the truth about witchcraft in western society. In 1969, the *Encyclopedia* finally printed a retraction of her theory, acknowledging that it was not accepted or supported by academic authorities—but that did little to lessen public belief in her ideas. One of the people who believed Margaret Murray's ideas to be factual was Gerald Gardner, the founder of modern Wicca.

Gerald Brosseau Gardner (1884–1964) came from an upper-class British family. He lived overseas as a youth and became interested in local religious beliefs and practices in Southeast Asia. People falling into trance states and exhibiting other strange behaviors made a particular impression on him. He eventually wrote a book on the magical beliefs and practices of the peoples he spent time with. After he retired from his overseas work in 1936, he returned to England, where he joined an occult group called the Rosicrucians. Through this group, he claimed to have met and joined the New Forest coven in 1939, and he thought this coven was a surviving example of Margaret Murray's witch cult.

There were only so many occult groups in England at the time, so it is no shock that he met Aleister Crowley (1875–1947) in 1947. Crowley is probably the most famous occultist in the western world. His face was on a Beatles album cover; he is mentioned in a number of popular songs; and his personality and ideas are explored in many documentaries and books. There are endless criticisms and defenses of him; most of the defenses are strained and thin. We don't need to go into detail about what Crowley was up to and what he wrote: so much of it is simply too vulgar and shocking. One example, for our purposes, is his book of rituals for summoning demons: he clearly was interested in the demonic and in black magic. Gardner, for his part, clearly made a strong impression on Crowley, who was older and looking for a successor to lead his occult organization. But Gardner did not just want to inherit Crowley's empire; he wanted to create his own system.

Gardner combined Margaret Murray's imaginary witch cult with Crowley's black magic and some ideas from Freemasonry. He put his own spin on all of this and called his system witchcraft and the people who practiced it "wiccans." His system had a group of women, himself (conveniently) as the leader, and a secret black book of magic. He put a lot of emphasis on nudism, in which he had a general interest. He wisely left out being burned alive at the end of the year. A few women would later break off from his organization and form their own versions of witchcraft, with a more female-centered philosophy.

His system would have likely remained a footnote in history but for the media. He had written books and promoted his system, but it was the television interviews that brought the existence of modern witches into the public consciousness. The broadcast that likely had the largest impact was a BBC interview in 1957 titled "Out of Step: Witchcraft." He was interviewed by an investigative journalist named Daniel Farson. Gardner brought the folk tales of witchcraft into the modern world and asserted that witches were alive and active in England, sparking fascination. Meanwhile, Margaret Murray's witch-cult theory remained in the *Encyclopedia Britannica* for twelve more years.

Witchcraft would go on to be featured in many films of the 1960s and 1970s. This certainly led many people to research witchcraft, and they found either Murray's theories themselves or other accounts based on her work. The movie screen is a powerful force, and by the end of the 1960s, when the witch-cult idea had been debunked as fabrication, the witchcraft created by Gerald Gardner had bloomed into actual practice. It carried with it the false claims of being an ancient woman-centered religion, as opposed to a mix of historical nonsense and nineteenth-century occultism created by men who enjoyed having a lot of women around to have sex with.

Today, the horse has long since left the barn, and there are thousands of books on witchcraft. Some are derivative of Gerald Gardner's system, while others are so many iterations away from his work as to be completely unrelated. Most witchcraft and Wicca still use false claims of ancient origins to gain an air of legitimacy, though some do not. Some are more open about being made up, even encouraging each practitioner to make up his or (usually) her own ideas and rituals. In many cases, the only remaining trait is that there are rituals designed to bring about the will of the practitioner.

What follows is one of my first encounters with real witchcraft.

Ed Warren was a layperson who assisted people with haunted homes from the 1950s until shortly before his death in 2006. He also worked with a number of people who may have been possessed. The cases Ed worked on are controversial, like the "Amityville Horror" case. Ed is also controversial himself, as he claimed to have amassed compelling evidence that proves the supernatural—but skeptical reviews of the evidence usually ended in unfavorable conclusions. Some criticisms are also reasonable from a Catholic perspective, such as his use of trance mediums to talk with spirits: mediumship is forbidden by the Church and specifically in the Bible, and talking with (as opposed to demanding answers from) demons is always a bad idea. Ed did work with legitimate exorcists, but he also worked with schismatic clergy.

After the Second Vatican Council (1962–1965), many things changed in the way priests were trained in seminary. Exorcism and spiritual warfare faded into obscurity in the United States; there were only a handful of exorcists operating, usually far from public awareness. Ed and his wife, Lorraine, tried to fill this gap during a time when the Church was often less responsive.

Ed had a protégé named John, who grew up knowing Ed and developed an interest in his unusual work. When John turned eighteen, Ed let him accompany and learn on cases. Over the years, John learned a lot about haunted-house cases and attended some exorcisms. Like Ed, John knew priests in the Catholic Church as well as clergy who were affiliated with other sects.

I met John when he gave a talk at a paranormal conference at Penn State in 2005. He had been working in the paranormal field for about thirty years at that point. After his talk, I went up to meet him. We had some more time to talk that evening, and not long after, I drove up to stay at his house for a few days. I learned about his history with Ed Warren and the somewhat underground network of people who had tried to help the public in the decades the Church was less active. When I visited, we would go out on cases that John had lined up. This is one of them.

Pam, a mother of three girls who lived in Maine, was desperate for help. Strange things had been happening in the house, but the strangest of all were the words that had become mysteriously scratched into her skin. Needless to say, she was worried for her young children. Pam's mother also lived with the family, but she did not seem to be involved in the matter.

Pam had arranged to have her girls elsewhere when we visited. We talked with her and learned about her background. John and I saw some witchcraft-related toys around, but Pam denied being involved in the occult, except a bit when she was younger. We wondered if she was oppressed or possessed. She walked us around the house and showed us where things had happened; upstairs, we ran into her mother. In the basement there was a very large and curious stone, too heavy to move, that had some symbols scratched into it: symbols that could have been notable or just some random marks. John then wanted to walk the yard. While he was behind the house, John spotted something odd hidden under the swooping branches of a low tree: we saw what looked like three child-sized graves with little mounds of disturbed dirt. We took sticks and made sure there was nothing buried there, then asked Pam about the mounds. She knew nothing about them, but naturally she found it disturbing. Pam asked her mother if she had seen the mounds, but she also said she had not.

John had brought a priest friend with him in case there was a need to pray over someone. Pam wanted any prayers that might help stop whatever was scratching her and causing problems in the house. She was sitting in the living room near John and the priest as Father started to pray. I was standing a bit back, holding a large crucifix and silently praying in support as best I could. About five minutes into the prayer, we heard a loud and commanding voice burst forth, "Get out of my house!"

Everything stopped, and I slowly turned to the voice behind me. I saw Pam's mother standing in a purple robe with a short crowbar in one hand and what looked like a cannonball in the other hand. The voice that came out of her did not sound like her. Everyone stood still. She looked me in the eye with anger, then at the crucifix I was holding, back at my eyes, and back at the crucifix. The pry bar and heavy ball clattered to the floor, then she ran upstairs. Everyone jolted into action. Pam stood and shouted, "She tried to burn the house down before, we have to stop her!"

We ran upstairs, but the mother had locked herself in her room. Pam tried to call her through the door, but there was no response. The house was old, and the doors were sturdy. I advised Pam to call an ambulance while we tried to stabilize the situation. We quickly asked Pam many questions about her mother, her habits, her history, and if she had had similar outbursts in the past. At first, she only said that she has episodes where she does not seem to be herself. Then she explained that her mother had been the head of a coven of thirteen witches for years. We told Pam it would have been helpful to have told us this earlier.

The ambulance came, along with the police. They broke into the mother's room and took her to the ambulance. She walked with them without resistance. When she was about to get into the ambulance, she turned to look back at the house and at us. She put a large, exaggerated smile on her face and slowly waved goodbye.

We went up to her room and found pictures of her three grand-daughters on the floor, along with some occult objects. Pam was very upset at this point. We realized that if her mother was possessed, she would act completely normal at the medical evaluation and be home in an hour or less. The demons would want to get back home as soon as possible. We quickly blessed the house thoroughly, and I did the Epiphany Blessing of the Threshold on the entry doors of the house. Pam left to go to the relative's house where her daughters were staying, and we left as well.

A few months later, Pam called John to tell him what had happened after that day. Her mother had been released from the hospital after only forty-five minutes. When she got home, she could not enter the house. When she tried to cross the threshold, she stopped breathing and had to retreat outside. Pam had to rent a trailer for her to live in the yard. Then, one of her daughters was scratched badly in front of her—frighteningly enough that Pam packed them in her car and drove to Florida. They left half-eaten bowls of cereal on the kitchen table. Pam had the contents of the house auctioned off, and she started a new life. We never learned what became of her mother.

Chapter 4

The Wandering Possessed

A kind and devout Catholic family took in an eighteen-year-old homeless girl who had befriended one of their daughters. Over the next few weeks, their daughter and the girl spent more and more time together in the basement, where the parents had set up a bed for her. They suspected the girl had a drug problem, and they offered to pray for her or to get her professional help. She refused both.

At dinner one night, they were praying as a family and the girl started violently shaking her head, as if to say "no, no, no." When they asked if she was alright, the girl angrily muttered something and went to the basement. The family called for help from a priest, and I was along for the visit.

When we pulled into the driveway in the early evening, the homeless girl retreated to the basement, even before we approached the house and knocked. As we talked with the family, she remained downstairs. The daughter who had befriended her said the girl did not want anything to do with us. The parents were concerned about the girl and how their family seemed to be more and more irritable during her stay. Additionally, they had been hearing strange noises in the house.

As the house was being blessed, I went to do the Epiphany Blessing of the Threshold. It seemed like a strong movement of grace happened during that prayer. After some more discussion, we left, since the homeless girl refused to come out of the basement. The parents, for their part, could not bear the idea of kicking her out, since it seemed uncharitable to do so. We packed up our things and left at the end of the evening.

The next day, the parents called to update us. A few minutes after we left, the homeless girl packed her things and told the family, "My friends had to leave and they can't come back. I'm leaving." With that, she walked out and the family never saw or heard from her again.

Chapter 5

Pray for Deliverance!

In the early years of my work with the spiritual world, I knew very little about deliverance prayers or exorcism. I knew about possession and that there was a kind of secret world going on all around us, but I did not know much about how to help. I was not yet working for the Church full-time, so I would go along with paranormal groups, or with John (Ed Warren's protégé), or with others. There were many young hobby groups at that time, but there were also people who had been dedicated to sincerely trying to help, rather than simply to gather data and leave, like most groups do.

I was along on a house case in a major city. The family complained of the typical problems: unexplainable black shadows moving through the house, strange noises, and things going missing and then reappearing in strange places. In addition, the woman who owned the house was waking up with scratch marks and bruises on her. She did not think she was accidentally hurting herself in her sleep.

After the house blessing, the woman actually felt worse. She said that while I was doing the blessing, she felt increasingly tense and afraid. Then she had sharp pains in her back and shoulders, and she found fresh, shallow scratch marks on her skin. She had been with us the entire time, and the scratches were where she could not reach. I said that we should pray for her, and we started praying the Psalms. The woman had been kind, reasonable, and appreciative all that day; there was nothing unusual or disquieting about her.

Suddenly, she bellowed in a commanding tone, "Pray for deliverance!"

Then, a moment later, she seemingly startled back awake and said in her regular voice, "That wasn't me. What happened?"

I knew generally what the word deliverance meant, but I was unfamiliar with charismatic prayer or deliverance prayer. Nonetheless, I said that we should pray for deliverance. I did my best to pray, asking Jesus to deliver her of whatever was attacking her. I don't recall the words I used, since it was almost fifteen years ago, but I know that a peace settled over the home and the woman. As far as I know, she was delivered, as I did not hear about her case again.

Part II

Learning the Ropes

*In which I really begin to understand the
seriousness of what I am being called to do*

Chapter 6

Sold His Soul for Rock 'n' Roll

I knew the myth that Robert Johnson, a great blues guitarist of the early twentieth century, had sold his soul to become an extraordinary musician. In two years, he went from being an amateur to a master of multiple styles of guitar playing; it was said that at a crossroads in rural Mississippi, he encountered the devil, who sold him his talent. Some of Robert Johnson's songs may have contributed to the legend, with names like "Hellhound on my Trail," "Me and the Devil Blues," and "Cross Road Blues." Some of these songs make direct reference to hellish figures, and other songs make veiled references to practices in African Hoodoo magic.

This story, a classic in rock 'n' roll lore, is just a legend. In reality, Johnson had been tutored by the talented Isaiah "Ike" Zimmerman over those two years. The references to the devil and hellhounds probably had more to do with the view some held at the time that the blues was the devil's music.

But that does not mean the devil does not seek out the talented or ambitious in order to tempt them with false promises of fame.

In 2007, we got a request from a mother about her son, who she said was possessed and dying. Apparently, he could not eat and had been huddled in the corner of their living room for a month. She put him on the phone, and he stammered in a weak voice that he wanted help, but that was all he could muster. It was a bitterly cold January, and I made the drive north into New York State to make an initial visit on my own. The house was run-down and close to the road on the outskirts of a small town. The mother answered the door. She was very brief and indicated where the living room was. She immediately went upstairs and left me alone. I walked into the dim living room and waited for my eyes to adjust. I did not see anyone: there was some old furniture, a dusty rug, and some framed prints on the walls. An old-fashioned tube TV sat dark. Then I saw what I first took to be a pile of laundry in the corner.

I walked halfway over and called out, "Matt, is that you?"

The pile of laundry shuddered and shifted.

"Yes," he croaked.

"It's Adam. Your mother asked me to come."

"Don't come near me, I don't want to hurt you," he said.

"Okay, can you tell me if you want help? Do you think you are possessed?"

His croaking noise turned into an animalistic growl, and he shuffled in my direction. Snarling and shaking his head side to side, he stammered out, "Stay away from me, I can't control it! Yes, I want help! Help me!"

"Okay Matt, I'm going to get help. I'll be back soon."

I could now smell the awful stench coming from him, like he had not bathed in a month or more. I could see that his clothes were so baggy that they were basically draped on him, like a garbage bag with sticks in it. I had never seen someone in such bad shape, other than maybe inmates brought into prison from living on the street. There was no more I could do that day, and his family was there to get emergency medical help for him if needed.

Over the next two weeks, until I could visit with an exorcist, Matt called many times, often in the middle of the night. Between my trying to calm him and reassure him, he told me his story. He said that there was a serious satanic cult in the small city near him and that his female cousin was in it. He was terrified of the cult, saying that they operated out of an industrial building in town and in caves by the river.

When he was seventeen, he had told his cousin that he wanted to get better at the guitar and to lead the classic rock 'n' roll life-style. She said she could show him how to get what he wanted, and he agreed to do a black magic ritual in which he offered himself in exchange for the ability to play the guitar—and all the other pleasures that come with musical success.

Within a short time, he began touring with a dark metal band. He seemed to have gotten what he wanted. But after seven years, everything was pulled out from under him, and he found himself back home living with his parents, broke, possessed, and dying from lack of nutrition. He was tormented by demonic nightmares and images of being tortured in awful ways.

Matt's case was blessedly fast: after one exorcism, he seemed fine for a week. He ate, bathed, and slept normally for the first time in ages. Then there was a relapse; perhaps one demon had been hidden and not cast out. There was a second exorcism, and the final demon came out easily.

Matt still calls me once a year or so to let me know he is doing well.

Chapter 7

The Divining Rods

Molly was a somewhat well-known person in the early paranormal community. Her specialty was using "divining rods" either to indicate where spirits were or to get answers from spirits by the moving of the rods.

Divining rods are a modern version of what "water witches" used to do with a forked stick. The idea was that the stick would point down when above an underground water source. Modern attempts to verify this supposed ability have shown that they perform no better than chance. Modern divining rods are often two small L-shaped metal rods held lightly in one's hands. When the rods swing and cross over each other, it is said to indicate a positive result of some kind. Some people interpret them swinging apart to mean something, as well. Molly's apparent gift was to detect where spirits were and to communicate with them using the rods.

I had met her at a paranormal conference, and she appeared to not like me very much; she did not appreciate my critical stance on ghost hunting. This was fine and not unusual, since I spoke at conferences about how ghost hunting is actually dangerous because only demons are going to respond to attempts at spirit communication. I did not see her or hear about her for a number of years after that.

Then, one day, Molly contacted me out of the blue and asked if we could talk. She explained that she had been using the rods more over the years and that her "gift" had intensified. But then she felt like she was being told, like a very strong intuition, that she no longer needed to use the rods. She felt that she just had to give permission and she could detect spirits and talk with them herself. Molly thought this was a good thing, and she said yes. Her life then went downhill quickly.

Almost immediately, a voice began talking in her mind, giving her instructions all the time, not just when she was ghost hunting. Soon she started experiencing waves of electrical sensations in her body, and her dreams felt like they had been invaded by another personality. She started meditating and doing other New Age practices in an attempt to control these experiences, but that only seemed to intensify them. Molly started experiencing a strong impulse, like a command, to kill herself. She was being told that it would be better when she was dead and that she would be able to more fully communicate with spirits when she was one herself. She found herself fixating on this idea—and that is when she decided to contact me.

I drove to her that weekend. She now assumed that whatever was tormenting her was a demon and that it was furious with her. In fact, it had said that she should kill herself before I came to visit, and then she felt its wrath focus on me when I arrived. I prayed the Litany of the Saints, as I always do. After the second time through the Litany, whatever was oppressing Molly broke and left. She suddenly had peace and quiet in her mind for the first time in months. She immediately said she was going to learn all she could about Jesus and dedicate her life to thanking Him for saving her. As far as I know, she continues to do well and has never returned to ghost hunting.

Chapter 8

A Psychic Kid

A child featured on a show about kids with supposed psychic abilities became one of my cases. The little girl had had negative experiences with what she thought were spirits most of her life. She participated in the show, and in the process she was coached to open up more to spirits and their manifestations—including negative ones. Her family is Protestant Christian, but psychic sensitivity seemed to run in the family and was normal to them.

On the night that her episode aired, the whole extended family was there to watch and celebrate her being on TV. During the show, however, she collapsed on the floor, started contorting, and spoke foul language and blasphemies in a male voice. Her family was shocked and terrified.

The child's mother contacted me and asked if I would come and try to help her. The daughter also said she wanted help. They had asked their local Catholic parish, but the pastor was not comfortable coming to the house. The minister of their own denomination was the girl's grandfather, but he was uncomfortable praying with her after what he saw. After making sure they had taken her to her doctor to be checked out, I agreed to come and to talk with her and the family.

When I arrived, several members of the extended family were there. The child explained her previous life experiences, what doing the show was like, and that she blacked out sometime during the airing of the episode. She said that since then, she was seeing black shadowy figures, hearing blaspheming voices, and being told to kill her mother. She also had periods of lost time, after which she returned to her senses in a different room, or outdoors, or in someone else's house.

After asking a lot of questions and hearing the whole story, I asked her grandfather, their minister, if he wanted to pray over her. He said no, that he would rather I do that. I explained that I'm only a layperson, but they insisted, and the girl was happy to be prayed for. I suggested that we start by blessing the house thoroughly, since it had not been blessed in the past. The mother took me around the house while everyone else stayed in the living room. The daughter's room was in the poorly lit basement with dark paneling. While there with her mother, I took holy oil and made several small crosses on the walls, ceiling, and hidden under the bed and behind the nightstand. In total, there were sixteen crosses.

We then went back to the living room to rejoin the family. The daughter looked different. She was staring hard at me with hatred in her eyes. She leaned back into the couch and then arched her back upward, like a suspicious cat. Her hands were clawed and digging into the cloth of the couch. I sat down next to her, with her mother on the other side, and gently started praying the Litany of the Saints while touching her shoulder. She started making odd noises and whispering, "no," over and over. After about fifteen minutes of prayer, she suddenly went limp and silent; when she came to, she seemed better. She said that things were quiet and she felt peaceful. We prayed a bit more, and there was no more reaction. I packed up and started the long drive home.

A week later, the mother called me. Her daughter was struggling again and had started speaking in this other voice more often. She had not gone back into her room since my last visit, saying in an angry voice that she wouldn't go "in the box of sixteen crosses." She asked if I could come back, since she was not sure she could physically control her small daughter much longer. I agreed to come the next day.

This time, fewer members of the family were there, and the mother sat on the other side of the kitchen table from her daughter. As I prayed the Litany, the spirit fully manifested again and started to say mean things to me and to her mother. Her mother yelled for it to get out of her daughter. At one point, this male voice said something like, "Fine, if you don't want me!" and the daughter went limp. She came to her senses, and again she said things were quiet. This time, she was able to return to her bedroom, and she had no further manifestations in the subsequent years. All of her "psychic" abilities also disappeared when the demon left.

Chapter 9

"Coward!"

I was asked to go to New York City to help a family troubled by manifestations in their apartment. It was a long drive, and I arrived around noon. There were two older sisters with adjacent apartments, one lived alone and the other lived with her adult son; the son hated his aunt and lived in a back room.

I interviewed the sister who lived alone, who was the one experiencing the troubles. She would see a white mist moving through the apartment, had strange repetitive dreams, saw strange things in mirrors, and once heard a voice say, "Breathe me in," as a white mist tried to enter her mouth and nose while she was going to sleep. She was frightened and had a feeling it was related to her nephew.

The other sister lived downstairs in a larger apartment with some big dogs. She explained that her son had gotten involved in Wicca and was doing some dark things. He had gotten meaner recently, she said, and he did not want her to have me over. In fact, he specifically told her to not have the apartment blessed. She responded that it was her apartment, and she would decide. She then explained to me that he was at work, and that she had chosen this day and time so he could not interfere.

I started by blessing and praying for the troubled sister and her apartment. That seemed to go by without incident. Then we started praying in the other sister's apartment. About five minutes into saying the house blessing, there was a rattling at the door and the son burst in—more than two hours before his shift was supposed to end. I kept praying and did not turn around, and the two sisters kept praying as well. The son stomped loudly toward me from behind. He approached and whispered, "Coward!" harshly in my ear and then went to his room. I did not respond and kept praying. He slammed the door, and it sounded like he started tearing his room apart, smashing things against the walls. We kept praying and used holy water throughout the apartment. His mother looked scared and embarrassed. The son never came out of his room, but we could hear him continue to break things, mumbling and yelling something incomprehensible.

We finished the house blessing and prayed as a group for a short time. The noise from the son's room went quiet, but he did not come back out. The mother thanked me and said she would find a way to handle her son. I never heard an update, which is not uncommon, but I'm hopeful the family was able to come together and heal.

Part III

The Big Leagues

In which I begin to advise during solemn exorcisms, get to know several demons, and see just about everything they are capable of

Chapter 10

Welcome to the Big Time, Kid

During my early years working on cases in Pennsylvania and New England, I had met one or two older exorcists who worked in the big cities. There was usually one exorcist for a large city, and their job was kept confidential even among the priests of their diocese. Eventually, though, I learned of an exorcist who lived relatively close to me, and I'll never forget the first things he said to me.

"Do you have a wife?" he asked.

"No," I said.

"Do you have children?"

"No."

"Do you have pets?"

"No."

After a pause, he said, "Well, I suppose you can come and talk someday."

I lived a few cities away from this priest and was busy with graduate school. It would be some months before I made the drive to visit this priest. We talked for a long time about his work and my own experiences. We discussed an ongoing case of a possessed woman he was working on, and as the sun was setting he said, "Well, shall we go up town and meet her?"

I was surprised and a bit unsure, but I said yes. While I thought I had encountered a possessed person by accident years ago during that impromptu hypnosis session, this was different. This was an ongoing formal exorcism case that involved a psychiatric nurse, a medical doctor, a psychiatrist, and an exorcist. This was almost certainly the real thing.

We sat in the living room with the possessed woman and her husband. I sat across from the couch where the couple sat, and the exorcist was in another chair. As the husband told us about the history of her problem, I noticed the woman was staring at me with a hard look in her eyes. The exorcist calmly commented, "Oh, there it is."

While keeping his attention on his wife, the husband finished the story, including how no holy items could be kept in the house because they disappeared. By disappear he meant that they would place an object on the table, turn to talk to someone, then turn back and find it was gone. She sat next to him, unmoving, just staring at me. I felt strangely calm and was a little surprised at that. In my years of training in clinical psychology, we were taught to become acutely aware of our internal states, and here I was not feeling anxiety or fear. During a quiet pause in the conversation, I said, "Hello there." She just kept staring, but with a bit of wary unease. As an aside, the exorcist commented to the husband with a bit of surprise, "He's not afraid of her."

This case had been going for years before this visit, and the diagnosis was long since over. Some of the details of that diagnosis, however, were related to me. When several priests were present who spoke different languages, the woman was questioned in English, French, Latin, Lithuanian, and German. She grew up on a farm, had a high school education, and only spoke English. Regardless, she either spoke or correctly answered all the questions. She also could correctly tell if something was blessed just by looking at it. The sign of unusual strength was shown in the actual exorcisms, where it sometimes took five healthy men to keep her restrained, and even then, she never tired over multiple hours.

Since the demon had manifested, it was decided to end the conversation and see if the woman could be brought back to her senses. This was not a day when a solemn exorcism was planned, which required a whole group of people to be present. The exorcist and I drove back to the rectory while the husband did whatever he had learned to do with his wife in this state. The exorcist explained that if things got difficult, the husband would call and we would go back, but praying and addressing the demon now would only agitate it and likely lead to physical attacks by her, possibly for hours. By removing the agitating factor—the exorcist and me—she likely would settle down on her own. Meanwhile, I found myself wondering about the intense scrutiny the demon seemed to have subjected me to.

We talked a bit and had dinner. A session was planned for the next day, and the exorcist asked if I wanted to come. Several other people would be there, and I could help restrain the woman along with her husband. I agreed.

The next afternoon, we went to the couple's home. Her primary care physician, her sister (a psychiatric nurse), her husband, and I were the team assisting the exorcist. This time when I came into the house, the woman seemed to be herself. She shook my hand, said hello, and thanked me for coming. She sat on the couch, while her sister sat next to her, holding her hand. The exorcist asked if I would sit on the other side and hold her other hand. The husband knelt and leaned forward a bit, getting ready to hold her legs.

The exorcist explained that he expected everyone to make the responses to the prayers if they knew them, and everyone needed to respond during the Litany of the Saints. About twenty saints into the Litany, the woman seemed to fall unconscious. I noticed her sister got a good grip on her hand and forearm, so I tried to do the same, but I was not as sure how best to hold a person.

The woman's eyes opened, and her face slowly turned toward the exorcist, her teeth bared. She hissed and pulled forward with both arms, straining toward the priest. I got a better hold off her right hand, but it twisted and turned, trying to get free or get a grip on my fingers. The husband was struggling hard against her legs, which were kneeing him in the chest and partly lifting him up. We all faltered in saying the responses to the prayers. The exorcist paused and firmly told us to keep praying. The woman writhed and growled, trying to reach a hand forward toward the purple stole that hung across the priest's neck and down in front of him. She turned her head toward the sister and focused on wrestling with her for a few moments, then turned toward me with an almost happy gleam in her eye. A wicked smile spread across her face, and she looked at the husband and kneed him harder in the chest, using both legs to push him back.

This continued until we completed the Litany. The exorcist then started on the old solemn exorcism rite (the new 1999 Rite of Exorcism had not come out yet), which had been written in 1614 and has been in continuous use since.[4] There are Gospel readings, Psalms, and large sections of exorcism prayers and commands to the demon. The rite essentially has three phases: prayers to agitate and wear the demon down, interrogations to get answers to questions, and adjurations to command it to leave the person.

---

[4] The old exorcism rite was never officially translated into English, so these are approximate and unofficial translations of the rite that can be found in the Roman Ritual of 1952.

An example of an agitation is the reading from the Gospel of John that reminds the demon that he is a creature, created by the Word of God. It reminds him that he is not God, and that he is not in charge:

> In the beginning was the Word, and the Word was with God, and the Word was God. The same was in the beginning with God. All things were made by Him, and without Him was made nothing that was made. In Him was life; and the life was the light of men: and the light shineth in darkness, and the darkness comprehended it not.[5]

Here is an example of interrogation—note all of the acts of God invoked in the question:

> I command thee, unclean spirit, whosoever thou art, along with all thine associates who have taken possession of this servant (handmaid) of God, that, by the mysteries of the Incarnation, Passion, Resurrection, and Ascension of our Lord Jesus Christ, by the descent of the Holy Spirit, by the coming of our Lord unto judgment, thou shalt tell me by some sign or other thy name and the day and the hour of thy departure.[6]

The questions are limited to who the demon is, how the demon and his associates got in the person, and when Jesus had decreed that they will leave. Any further questioning would be for the sake of curiosity, not for the good of the possessed, and so is not allowed. Further, anything outside of what is prescribed by the Church does not carry the Church's authority, so the demon can

---

[5] *The Roman Ritual*, vol. II (New York: Bruce, 1952), 179.
[6] *Roman Ritual*, vol. II, 179.

lie and use the questioning to draw the interrogator into deceptions. The reason the demons have to answer truthfully to the authorized questions, even though they are liars by nature, is the authority Jesus gave His Church over demons. Even when an exorcist has apostolic authority from and through his bishop, the demons may resist for a time; but eventually they get spiritually worn down and they answer.

Here is an example of adjuration, which conveys some of the force and poetic style of the old rite of exorcism:

> I cast thee out, thou unclean spirit, along with the least encroachment of the wicked enemy, and every phantom and diabolical legion. In the name of our Lord Jesus Christ, depart and vanish from this creature of God. For it is He Who commands thee, He Who ordered thee cast down from the heights of heaven into the nethermost pit of earth. He it is Who commands thee, Who once ordered the sea and the wind and the storm to obey. Hence, pay heed, Satan, and tremble, thou enemy of the faith, thou foe of the human race! For thou art the carrier of death and the robber of life; thou art the shirker of justice and the root of all evil, the fomenter of vice, the seducer of men, the traitor of the nations, the instigator of envy, the font of avarice, the source of Discord, the exciter of sorrows![7]

When the actual exorcism prayers began, the woman's fighting became much more intense. I was surprised at her strength; it was a real struggle to keep up with her. I saw that her sister, who had a lot of practice, was doing better. The husband looked like he was having a hard time. The exorcist was standing behind the

---

[7] *Roman Ritual*, vol. II, 185.

husband while overlooking the scene. The woman started sliding down the couch as she pushed her husband back; we could not lift her back into a sitting position. "If we go to the floor, just stay with that arm," the exorcist told me.

It seemed the husband could not control her legs anymore, and he started to pull her the rest of the way off the couch and onto the carpet. We moved with her, and her sister put a hand behind her head as we slid her down to the floor. I saw why a few seconds later, as the woman lifted her head as far as she could and tried to slam the back of her head on the floor. Her sister controlled this as best she could, using her own hand to cushion the blow. The husband shifted around, laying across her legs and hugging her waist, putting all his weight on his wife's midsection, attempting to hold her still.

I attended dozens of exorcisms in this case, which seemed to settle into a kind of standoff. The demons stopped manifesting strongly and sat motionless during the exorcisms, not speaking. They also stopped manifesting during the week, and the woman resumed much of her life activities. Some cases just do not resolve for many years, and we do not always know why.

Chapter 11

The Demons on Brownsville Road

When I was still approaching demonic cases from a psychological and brain science perspective, I was asked by the Diocese of Pittsburgh to go along with a team to the famous Cranmer house on Brownsville Road in the South Hills of Pittsburgh.[8] The family had lived there since the 1980s, but the father of the family, Bob, had been drawn to the house since he was a child growing up in the area. After moving in, the manifestations slowly progressed from smaller to greater: crucifixes were chewed on; black shadows were seen moving through the home; voices called from the basement; light fixtures and walls had what looked like blood spattered on them. A local priest had been working with the family and praying over the home for some time. My role was to provide a psychological take on the family members, as well as to make a general impression of the case. My first visit was in early 2005.

---

[8] Unlike all of the other cases discussed in this book, the identifying details of this case are not changed. This is because the case has been published in a book by the head of the family: Bob Cranmer and Erica Manfred, *The Demon of Brownsville Road: A Pittsburgh Family's Battle with Evil in Their Home* (New York: Berkley Books, 2014).

Bob Cranmer, the father of the family, took me around the house as soon as I arrived. He took me to the closet under the stairs where manifestations first started when the pull chain for the closet light became unaccountably tangled. Then one day, he found it tied in knots. Bob put a rosary around the light and soon found the crucifix disfigured by what looked like teeth marks. After that, strange things started happening in other parts of the house. After he walked away, I paused for a moment, feeling a certainty that something important was under the stairs. I quietly said, "You're in there. You're in there."

I rejoined Bob. He showed me the living room where Mass had been said on a weekly basis for years as an attempt to stop the manifestations. He said he found a Mass kit when he moved into the house, which isn't completely out of the ordinary in a Catholic city like Pittsburgh, but still unusual, since home Masses are fairly rare. Sometimes during Mass, he explained, they feel the evil presence being boldly present near them. We then went upstairs, where he showed me the various bedrooms of the home. Then we looked at the apartment in the attic space, where a number of people had heard and seen strange manifestations. On the way back down, he pointed out the red drips and stains on the wallpaper. These, he said, appeared the day after a house blessing when holy water had been sprinkled on the walls. He also pointed out reddish-brown stains on some of the antique light fixtures.

It was now evening, and I was sitting talking with someone on the second floor. I observed what looked like black blobs about three inches long glide along the floor, walls, and ceiling. (If you've ever seen the "soot sprites" in My Neighbor Totoro, that's the idea.) There were three or four of them moving around the room smoothly. I inspected the light coming in from the window and tested the direction of shadows from trees outside. I could not account for these black shadows, particularly on the unlit walls and ceiling.

I went downstairs and talked with Bob about my feeling that there was something important about the closet under the staircase. The staircase turns ninety degrees twice, which creates an open space under it that is partly utilized by the closet—but there was clearly more space beyond the back wall. After some consideration, Bob agreed and got out his circular saw, cutting a large opening in the wall. As far as we could tell, the space under the stairs had never been opened before. The construction looked uniform, and everything was coated with coal dust—very Pittsburgh.

We found a number of interesting things in that space, such as signatures from the builders of the house. Then we found a brittle piece of folded paper in the soot against the wall on the floor. Bob carefully unfolded it. On one side there was a crude picture of two houses with a road and a sunset with two women looking and smiling. On the back was the name of the family that had built the house: Malack. In addition, there were about four small toys belonging to Bob's kids, which had been lost during their childhoods. We looked as well as we could, and there did not seem to be any gaps in the construction for the items to fall through. One was a die, another was a Lego man. There was also a playing card that could have slipped between two boards.

Then it was time to interview Bob's sons, David and Bobby. I was sitting in a small parlor room with David, taking notes about his experiences in the house growing up. He was a bright and fit young man, and he did not seem dishonest or mentally ill. All of a sudden, he stopped, looked at me, and asked, "Do you want to know what the face of God looks like?" He then abruptly stood up, said he had to go, and walked out of the room.

There were other somewhat odd interactions with the family members, and it was becoming clear either that living in the house all those years had an effect on them, or that there were some difficult psychological dynamics in the family. There was no overt mental illness: they were all functioning in life and maintaining relationships with others. But there were strange moments that indicated that something wasn't quite right. Over the next day, I finished interviewing the rest of the family and then departed.

Two weeks later, I made a second visit to the home. This time it was snowing hard and had become quite cold. During this visit, my focus was more on observing the house and the way the people lived in it and interpreted events. I was trying to see how much of their experience might be misinterpretation or self-suggestion. I was also curious if there were genuine manifestations going on, such as the small shadows I had seen on my first visit.

I spent a fair amount of time quietly observing the family and the home, listening for settling noises, or how the furnace sounds when it starts up, or how the ductwork sounded when it cooled. At one point, I took a walk with two other people for a break; it was still snowing and a pretty winter night in Pittsburgh. After walking a few blocks from the house, there was a lightning strike, and the power went out in the surrounding neighborhood—except for the four street lights immediately around us. I'm sure it was an odd coincidence, but it had an unreal feeling when it happened.

After coming back to the house, I went into a room alone to think. I pictured the house and how it was built, like a blueprint or cross-section. In my imagination, I saw what looked like spirits moving in the house. I then had the strange sense of being looked back at. I went back to join the others and suddenly felt dizzy and a bit sick. They saw welts rise up on my forehead as if someone had scratched me with their fingernails. They quickly took some pictures. Soon I felt normal again, and then after about sixty seconds, the welts completely disappeared. Now, there is some psychological literature from the 1960s that showed that the mind can create welts and reddened skin just from hypnotic suggestion. But there was no hypnotist or other attempt at hypnosis in the house that night.

At the end of the second night of this visit, we decided to pray. These were just general prayers, including some informal prayers to free the home and family of anything that might be tormenting them. For some reason, these prayers felt very intense, and I had the *very* strong sense of a large angel being present who was very protective. After the prayers were done, there was a sense of some good having been accomplished, but also of something being angry. I thought of my family and prayed for protection for me and them. I felt like this prayer was granted, but that this came with expectations. The next morning, I left.

The case was resolved when an experienced exorcist from another diocese came in, with permission from the bishop, to exorcise the home. After that, by all accounts, everything stopped, and the family has enjoyed the house, and each other's company, since.

Chapter 12

Bad Gravy

Luis had grown up in Italy with a devout Catholic family. He felt he had a vocation to the monastic life since he was a boy; he hoped to dedicate himself totally to being with God. When he was in his late twenties, he moved to the United States for a good job opportunity, though he still hoped to find a way to live out the vocation to the religious life. In his first year in America, he met a young woman, and they started dating. She was not Catholic, but she was open to learning about the faith because of him. She agreed that if they married, they would raise their children Catholic. A year later, they were engaged, and soon after, they were married.

Luis's wife had been going with him to Mass and even started the RCIA (Rite of Christian Initiation for Adults) program. After a few months of marriage, however, she showed less and less interest in going to Mass or RCIA. They ended up having three children, but two of them his wife would not allow to be baptized. Then he discovered she had been having an extended affair. He tried to reconcile with her and suggested couples therapy—and to see a priest—but she refused. For the sake of the children, they maintained a civil friendship, but decided to file for divorce when it was clear that his wife did not want to end her new relationship.

The process began in the fall, and it was clear the divorce would be finalized early the next year. His wife's mother suggested that they have one last Thanksgiving dinner together as a family. He agreed.

After Thanksgiving, and for the rest of the year, Luis developed headaches and stomach pains, but he attributed these to the stress of the divorce and the financial strains involved. In January, the divorce was finalized, and he settled into work and would visit his children when he had visitation rights. But his wife only got more and more hostile toward him, and his older daughter did not want to spend time with him. Everything seemed to be collapsing.

Luis even started having trouble praying, which had always been important to him. When he would try to pray silently, his mind would go blank, and he would forget the words to prayers he had said thousands of times before. He found himself prone to uncharacteristic angry fits. Meanwhile, his mother back in Italy had been praying for him, along with a prayer group who had known Luis most of his life. In their prayer, they felt strongly that something more serious was wrong with Luis, and they encouraged him to have a priest pray over him.

Luis came in simply for deliverance prayers, since it looked like a simple case of oppression, or even just psychological troubles. We started the prayer session with the Litany of the Saints, which is also how exorcisms are started. During the Litany, Luis tensed up and clenched his fists. His eyes were closed and his face tensed, taking on a grimace of pain and rage. His hands started shaking, and he started muttering. As we continued to pray, the muttering turned into screaming. Seeing that something more was going on, we started performing the tests for possession.

Luis responded correctly to questions in Latin, Hebrew, and German. He may have had some previous knowledge of Latin, but he later confirmed that he knew neither Hebrew nor German.

At the beginning of the next session, we held a box of relics near him, and he could tell us the genders, descriptions, and, in some cases, names of the saints they came from. This all added up to a case of possession, so we obtained a psychological report from his doctor before proceeding.

The third session was a solemn exorcism. This time, Luis's reaction to what was going on around him was even stronger. Then, toward the middle of the exorcism, he started to wretch like he was going to throw up. It is not unusual for people to throw up, but it is more common for them to cough while being delivered from demons. (Demons are purely spiritual beings, but they sometimes have physical effects on matter.) In this case, he vomited up a dark brown and thick liquid that smelled absolutely terrible. Over the course of several sessions in the coming weeks, he would throw up more and more of the same substance. One day, it dawned on us what it looked like: dark turkey gravy. He said he had not eaten anything like that on the days of the sessions. As the process finally drew to a close, when the demons were commanded to tell the exorcist how they entered Luis, they said the turkey gravy was cursed by his mother-in-law at their Thanksgiving meal.

After about six months, the main demon associated with that Thanksgiving curse was cast out. The gravy never recurred. His case continued for some time, with many more major demons involved. They testified that Hell was fighting so hard for his case because they knew he had a vocation to religious life and that he loved God so much. Luis eventually took a job in a neighboring diocese and was transferred to their exorcist.

Chapter 13

Curses

Crystal grew up in a Catholic family. Her aunt had gotten involved in Wicca in the late 1970s and was still practicing it when Crystal was a youngster in the early 2000s. Her aunt made Wicca seem exotic and interesting, but Crystal never really tried it herself. Throughout her childhood and adolescence, Crystal continued to go to Mass regularly with her parents. But when she was a freshman in high school, there was a boy who had taunted her and her friends—so she looked up a spell to curse him and performed it. Her request was that he get sick and then apologize to her, but she did not take it too seriously and really did not think anything would happen.

The next morning, the boy was not in school, and Crystal learned he had gone to the hospital the previous evening with abdominal pain. Two days later, he returned to school, and the first time he saw her, he approached her and apologized for teasing her. He said that he would never tease her again—and, surprisingly, asked her to not hurt him again. This, understandably, had a significant impact on Crystal. That night, she threw away the book she had used and everything in the house related to Wicca.

Even so, since that day, she found herself not going to Mass. She was not opposed to it, but it always seemed there was some reason not to go or that something else came up. In fact, she did not attend Mass or Confession again for many years. She also never practiced black magic of any kind because she always felt bad for the boy she appeared to have harmed.

One may wonder how she was able to cause this harm and whether we need fear curses. If one is in a state of grace (no unconfessed mortal sin) then we generally do not need to fear curses. If one is in a state of spiritual death, having unconfessed mortal sin, we can be vulnerable. Curses seem most impactful when we eat or drink a cursed item, which is why saying grace over food is so important. In addition, Jesus allows effects to occur. In this case, the effect occurs to some extent, but was not permanently harmful. Before we jump to the conclusion that pain, psychological troubles, or bad luck is a curse, we should rule out the more likely mundane possibilities by seeing the appropriate professionals.

Crystal was twenty-six and living on her own. Her mother asked her to come to Mass for Christmas, since family was in town and it seemed like it had been forever since she had gone. Crystal went to Mass and truly enjoyed being there after so many years. But as she walked out of the church, she suddenly had a searing pain across her forehead. She touched her face and saw blood on her fingers. She checked in a mirror and saw three thin, shallow scratches across her forehead, which were bleeding in tiny droplets. Crystal had a twisting, sick feeling in her stomach and felt a rage that did not make sense to her. She had a sudden and deep feeling that something was very wrong.

Crystal called the diocese, and we discussed her background and the event after Mass. It seemed to be a likely case of demonic oppression, as she showed no signs of possession. She also seemed very reasonable and sane during the intake. When she arrived for prayer, she had an experience we have seen many times. As she stepped over the threshold, into the sanctuary where we pray, she started to shake uncontrollably and went very pale. Her eyes were glassy, and she struggled to speak. She said she definitely wanted prayer and to please start. We had her go to Confession so she could confess the sin of black magic intended to harm another, as well as any other sins.

We prayed deliverance prayers for about an hour, and she continued to shiver and sometimes twitch strongly during the prayer. At the same time, she was also very stiff. Afterward, she reported that she did not feel much better. We encouraged her to think if there was any other sin she might need to renounce, anything she had unforgiveness for, or anything else that may have opened a door. She said she wasn't sure, but she would think about it. We encouraged her to go to Mass that week a few times and certainly on Sunday.

The next week, she arrived for prayer a bit late and smelled of alcohol. She was pale and shaking again. Crystal told us that she had suddenly gotten an offer to transfer to another city for her company, and it would involve a raise, so she wouldn't be able to come for prayer again after that day. She also said she had tried to go to Mass but felt a distinct fear that she would be punished if she went, so she did not go. We prayed again, but she continued to be troubled. As she left that day, we strongly encouraged her to connect with the diocese where she was moving so the prayer sessions could continue. We never heard from her again, and we can only pray that she chose to fight her way out of the situation she had put herself in.

Chapter 14

The Pedophile Ghost

In the early years of my work, I was employed as a full-time psycho-logical services specialist in the Pennsylvania prison system, but I would sometimes be called to different dioceses to help with cases on the weekends. This time, I was told that a couple had become involved in paranormal investigating and gotten into trouble. I was asked to assess the situation.

I arrived at about eight in the evening to a city row house in a decent neighborhood. It was a cool fall evening, and the block was quiet. I grabbed my case with my prayer book, crucifix, holy water, blessed salt, and relics. The husband came to the door, looking a bit pale and stressed. He welcomed me, then apologized, saying that his wife had run upstairs a few minutes before I had arrived and wouldn't come down. As we started talking in the kitchen about the troubles his wife was having, I noticed her staring at me from behind the doorframe. She suddenly interrupted us in a flat tone, "He wants to know what's in the case." I said that if he's a spirit, then he already knows what's in the case. She replied, "He's afraid of what's in the case."

The husband got her to come into the kitchen and to sit down. She seemed pretty uncomfortable getting closer to me, but she complied. Her face was strangely blank, and she looked like she had been losing sleep. They explained that they had gotten interested in ghost hunting about six months ago and had joined a paranormal group. They had recently gone on a ghost hunt in a house where a pedophile had hung himself. The wife had stood where he died and invited him to talk to her while consciously trying to open herself completely in order to detect anything. She felt something rush into her, and that's when her problems started.

The wife lost the ability to express emotion in her face, and she felt like her internal experience of emotions was blunted. She lost interest in her hobbies and developed a sexual fixation on a sixteen-year-old boy in their paranormal group. All of this was alien to her personality, and it distressed her. She opened up to her husband, and he had noticed himself that her personality had dramatically changed. He took her to their doctor, and she underwent various tests, but no explanation could be found.

Then she said, "He knew when you were coming, about five minutes before you pulled up. He said we had to leave the house and run." I asked if she heard this voice talking to her since the ghost hunt, where she had tried to commune with the spirit. She said she did and that she could not control the voice or make it stop. I asked about their spiritual and religious background, as well as her medical and psychological history. I offered to pray to ask God to free her from this thing, and they enthusiastically agreed. I called in to my contact at the diocese and briefed them on the case, and they approved my prayer.

I simply prayed the Litany of the Saints, as I always did for spiritual problems. About half-way through the Litany, the wife let out a sudden cry and threw her arms around her husband. She was sobbing loudly and clutching him tightly. She said over and over that she was sorry, and she kissed his cheek and hugged him while he sobbed as well. I asked her if she still heard the voice, and she said no. Her expressions returned and she seemed clear in her thinking and speech. I finished the Litany to be sure, then packed up. I strongly advised them to stop ghost hunting, get rid of the equipment, and delete all the images, videos, and audio recordings they had collected—and they actually started bagging it all up into a garbage bag while I was preparing to leave. As far as I know, they had no further problems of that nature.

Chapter 15

Mark and Debby Constantino

I met Jay and Grant from the television show *Ghost Hunters* at a conference on the paranormal at Penn State in 2004. They listened to my talk at that conference and later suggested my name to other paranormal conference organizers, which opened a lot of doors for me. I soon met Mark and Debby Constantino, the most well-known experts on electronic voice phenomena (EVP) in the paranormal community.

The idea that spirits might use technology to communicate with the living is not new. In fact, it emerged from the most famous inventor in American history. In a 1920 interview, a seventy-three-year-old Thomas Edison said:

> I have been at work for some time building an apparatus to see if it is possible for personalities which have left this earth to communicate with us. If this is ever accomplished it will be accompanied not by any occult, mystifying, mysterious, or weird means, such as are employed by so-called mediums, but by scientific methods...
>
> I am hopeful, that by providing the right kind of instrument, to be operated by this personality, we can receive

intelligent messages from it in its changed habitation, or environment. If the apparatus I am constructing should provide a channel for the inflow of knowledge from the unknown world—a form of existence different from that of this life—we may be brought an important step nearer the fountainhead of all knowledge, nearer the intelligence which directs it all.[9]

No plans or any such device were ever found.

EVPs are said to be sounds left on a recording that were not audible during the actual recording—specifically sounds that could be voices. Unaccountable sounds on silent recordings were initially discovered by accident, then explored by a few different people around the world in the 1950s. Konstantin Raudive, a Latvian doctor, made more than a hundred thousand recordings of supposed EVPs and invented specialized equipment to record what he called Electronic Voice Projections. He tried to be scientific, using radio-shielded testing spaces and inviting other specialists to interpret his recordings. He wrote a book on his work that was published in 1968 and translated into English in 1971.[10] EVPs, along with photography, had supplanted the mediums and seances as the preferred way to discover and communicate with the spirit world.

The days of the Society for Psychical Research had passed, however, and the technological world had much less patience for these

---

9 Kristin Tablang, "Thomas Edison, B.C. Forbes and the Mystery of the Spirit Phone," *Forbes*, October 28, 2019, https://www.forbes.com/sites/kristintablang/2019/10/25/thomas-edison-bc-forbes-mystery-spirit-phone/?sh=1c917d0829ad.

10 Konstantin Raudive, *Breakthrough: An Amazing Experiment in Electronic Communication with the Dead*, trans. Nadia Fowler (California: White Crow Books, 2021).

notions. Spiritualism and attempts to document spirits had waned after the post-WWII boom. There was the Rhine Research Center at Duke University, which has since closed, that was still trying to document parapsychology, and a few other efforts elsewhere, but the general public was not at all aware of this work. When *Ghost Hunters* premiered in 2004, many people learned about and heard EVPs for the first time, thinking this technique and technology was new, not almost a century old.

The popular ghost hunting version of EVPs is very different from the laboratory work of Raudive and others. The process on the paranormal TV shows is to use a sensitive digital recorder in uncontrolled environments among groups of people. Radio interference, electrical interference, distant talking, and other factors are not controlled for—this is all hardly scientific.

In addition, the most popular recorders have it right in their user manuals that audible distortions are likely in low-volume environments. These recorders are usually set to self-adjust the microphone amplification depending on the ambient noise, so in a quiet environment the recorder turns up the gain on the microphone, amplifying noise, distortions, faint whispers, and distant talking. What is usually recorded and called an "EVP" are very faint sounds that may be similar to human speech. Often in recordings of several minutes or even hours, there are only a few syllables or maybe words captured. The various mundane (and obvious) possibilities are usually not tested for before declaring that the sound is paranormal in origin.

The two big problems with EVPs as they are done by casual operators are these: the equipment is usually prone to picking up slight radio signals and distortions, as we have said, and also that they do not account for the power of *pareidolia*, which is when the brain tries to find words in random noises, especially white noise.

The brain is an awesome pattern recognizer. It turns the sounds another person makes with his or her mouth into recognizable words, which we then decode into something meaningful. The brain is also very good at sifting through new inputs and connecting them to known patterns: this is why we can listen to someone talking in a thick accent, and after a little while, we start to understand them more clearly.

We can see this same phenomenon visually as we stare at clouds and resolve them into faces or animals. This is the basis of the famous Rorschach inkblot test: it is well established that we will see meaningful things in random stains of ink; it is what we see that tells the psychologist about our personality. In the same way, we can easily hear "words" in the static or distortions that generally make up EVPs. This is greatly enhanced when words are put on the screen along with the sounds, prompting the viewer to "hear" what he or she might not otherwise.

Mark and Debby appeared on a number of paranormal television shows, had regular blogs about the paranormal, and taught people how to capture EVPs at paranormal conferences. They were especially well known because they would consistently get voices on their recordings. Most people tried for hours and maybe got a few words, or none at all. What was especially troubling, though, was the nature of the voices they got.

As far as I know from talking with Mark and Debby, and from watching them do EVP recordings, the content of the voices they captured were almost always negative and usually directed toward Debby. Within thirty seconds of recording in any location, they would usually get what sounded like the same gravelly voice that would say things like, "Debby, I hate you," or "Die Debby!" Sometimes they seemed to get a few words from something neutral or even positive, but as far as I know, it always came back to hateful words in a threatening tone. They often used a recorder with a documented tendency to produce distortions, but other recorders would also produce the same voices for them.

As I got to know them, Mark and Debby confided to me that they had a number of spiritual manifestations in their home. Further, they did EVP recordings in their home, even though they said they knew this was not a good idea. In fact, they were Catholic, and so I explained to them that spirit communication is a violation of the First Commandment. They asked me to visit their house in Reno, since they felt that the manifestations were getting more hostile toward them. We talked for a long time, and they decided to stop doing recordings at home and even considered quitting EVPs altogether and committing to warning people about the potential dangers of ghost hunting. Unfortunately, they did not follow through on those good intentions.

About six months later, I got an early-morning call from Mark. I was at work at the diocese, and I was surprised to hear from him out of the blue. He sounded emotional and told me that I would be hearing some things about him soon, and he begged me not to judge him until the entire truth came out. I asked what he meant, assuming it was about some social drama in the paranormal community. He cried and said, "I guess the thing in the house is going to get what it wants." He hung up.

The next day, Mark first killed Debby's roommate, then her, and then himself at their daughter's apartment.[11] Mark and Debby had been recently estranged and had filed for divorce. I can't say

[11] Justin Wm. Moyer, "How Real-Life Horror Visited 'Rock Star' Ghost Hunters, Dead in Alleged Murder-Suicide," *Washington Post*, September 24, 2015, https://www.washingtonpost.com/news/morning-mix/wp/2015/09/24/how-real-life-horror-visited-rock-star-ghost-hunters-dead-in-alleged-murder-suicide/.

for sure that this tragedy occurred because of ghost hunting or EVPs—Mark may have been using them as an excuse for what he planned to do, or he may have been simply full of rage and confusion—but the coincidence of the threatening voices and Mark's last words to me have always left me wondering.

Chapter 16

What Are YOU Doing Here?!

In 2006, we hosted a conference on exorcism in Pittsburgh, and we brought in a European exorcist who had extensive experience, since there were few exorcists working in the United States in those days. I'll call him Fr. Joseph.

The conference seemed to go well. Fr. Joseph and I took some walks around town and had long conversations about theology, angels, and exorcism. Right after the conference, I drove Father to a different diocese for a difficult case I had been helping with for a few years, and I benefitted from his input. On the way back to Pittsburgh, we talked about the possibility of having me visit his country and spending a week or two learning from him.

I got my first passport and, in the winter of 2007, I flew overseas to stay with Father for seven days. We went to his parish, a small stone church with a very large stone baptismal font and the original high altar and fixtures, which were built in the 1200s. There were no electric lights, and the furnace was running minimally. He said Mass for the people, who all wore their winter coats and hats.

Father had explained that, over the years, he simply prayed with anyone who asked for deliverance prayers at the end of the day. There were so many cases brought to his parish from around his country that it was impractical to do a full evaluation of each one. On this day, there was one man who stayed after Mass. Father closed the doors of the Church and talked with him: it turned out he was from the capital city an hour away, and he felt that he was troubled by an evil spirit. This man could not speak more than a few words of English in a halting way and with a heavy accent.

The man was sitting in a pew toward the back of the small church. Father stood on one side of him and gestured for me to stand on the other side. Father started praying in his language, while I focused on praying the St. Michael prayer slowly, over and over. After a minute or so, the man started rocking forward and back in the pew, shaking and muttering. Father kept praying, looking to see if I noticed the reaction. Then the man turned to me with a look of surprise on his face, and yelled, "What are YOU doing here? Stop that praying! Stop it!"

He spoke in fluent English, with an American accent. Father looked up at me and raised his eyebrows in surprise. This was the first time I had really seen a facility in a language unknown to the person, so I was also surprised. That was all that he said, nothing more. We kept praying for about half an hour, but it did not look like the man was freed. Afterward, Father spoke to him in his own language for a while; it appeared that Father had asked the man to try to speak in his best English, because the man started trying to form an English sentence. He faltered and paused, unable to do so.

We saw multiple people that week, yet I found this incident disconcerting. It was the first time I had been personally recognized by a demon, and it felt especially striking for it to happen on another continent. Demons are spirits, of course, and distance does not have the same meaning for them, but it still was disturbing. I wondered what had caused me to be known to them. Perhaps it was helping to organize the conference? Maybe it was attending so many exorcisms? On one hand, it was an affirmation that I was doing something right, and on the other, it was a little unsettling to apparently be known by demons around the world.

Chapter 17

Little Girl "Ghosts"

There was a great deal of interest in the spiritual world during the Middle Ages. Perhaps the most well-known, if poorly understood, medieval text on the topic is the *Malleus Maleficarum* (*The Hammer of Witches*), published in 1486. The *Malleus* is mostly a collection of case notes from Inquisitors who were trying to make sense of the strange claims they were hearing—including stories of sexual intercourse with demons and resulting pregnancies.

The authors tried to resolve theological questions that arose from the phenomena people experienced. Were demons in any way physical, or purely spiritual? If they were not at all physical, how could they seem to move physical objects? Was it possible for spirits to impregnate people through what the subject experienced as sexual intercourse? If not, were they instead impregnating women by stealing sperm from a man and transporting it to a strange woman? Are the claimed pregnancies just lies or false pregnancies created by the minds of the women? The *Malleus* became the main source for the now well-known terms *succubus* and *incubus*. The succubus was a demon pretending to be a female who physically seduces a man to intercourse, and the incubus was a demon pretending to be a man and doing the same to women.

Usually these experiences are not physical, strictly speaking. These false experiences may feel real because they are somehow detected in the nervous system of the person. In other cases, it seems there is also physical movement of the person or of objects in the area. We do not know exactly how fallen angels can cause these physical effects, but it is clear that some can.

As shocking as it is, there are people who seek out such inter-actions. In the beginning, they are seeking pleasure, but as soon as they fully engage in the act, they enter into a particular union with the demon, who now has a claim on them. The interactions almost always cease to be pleasurable and become the opposite, unrelentingly. They are the ugliest type of cases we see. Here are two examples that should inspire adequate caution in the curious.

I once met an elderly exorcist in a major east coast city. He had gone to Rome for training in exorcism many years ago and had been the sole exorcist for this city for forty years. He was a joyful person and also very practical. We met over a case of a woman who was oppressed, but not possessed. Her case was serious, however, since she was being physically attacked by something in front of her children and husband.

The case had started when she was recovering in the hospital for a few days after an inpatient procedure. In the evenings, when it was quiet, she would hear what sounded like a little child walk-ing into her room and standing near her bed, wheezing a bit as it breathed. She took it to be the ghost of a little girl who had died in the hospital due to some respiratory problem. Her maternal instincts kicked in, and she verbally invited the ghost to come home with her when she was discharged.

When she got home, she told her children and husband about the ghost of the little girl she had invited home. They were inter-ested, and the whole family started talking to the "ghost." They would put children's toys out and encourage the little girl to move them, which it did. It would roll a ball or move stuffed animals. The family was impressed and encouraged more manifestations. Then, over the days and weeks, the presence started to feel larger than a little girl. The ghost felt more male than female, and it stopped playing with the toys. Then there seemed to be three spirits and not one, and the attacks started. The woman seemed to be physically held by two of the spirits and sexually attacked by the third. To the horror of the family, this occurred in front of them, but there seemed to be nothing they could do to stop it.[12]

It was at that point they called for help and were connected with Father. He was good at asking questions, trying to debunk events, and then addressing what he judged to be genuine spiritual problems. He took the time to teach the family about good and bad angels and God's rules for how we should not interact with the bad ones. Father also explained the common trick of posing as a child, as that makes people drop their guard. After everyone was clear on rejecting these deceptive spirits, he prayed over the family. As with many incubus and succubus cases, it did not resolve in one prayer session. In fact, this case did not resolve in the time that I was connected to it.

---

[12] One may again ask how angels can have physical effects, since they are purely spiritual beings. St. Thomas Aquinas wrestled with this question because the Old Testament describes angels as having bodies, eating, and being seen and heard. Abraham receives three angelic guests (Gen. 18:1–8); two angels visit Lot in Sodom, talk with him, and eat (Gen. 19). The New Testament describes angels appearing to Peter in prison and releasing him from his chains, having very physical effects (Acts 12). In the end, Thomas maintains that angels do not have bodies naturally united to them, but that angels sometimes assume bodies (*ST* I, 51, 1–2).

Later, Father asked me to take a different oppression case, with similarities to this one. I went to visit Brad at his apartment in the city. He lived austerely, with few pieces of furniture and no television. The hardwood floors were all bare. He was an intense, and tense, man. He explained that he had been under spiritual attack for many years: he was a trained nurse, but he could manage to work only about four hours a week. Brad had been to innumerable charismatic prayer groups and many priests for prayer, and he went to Mass almost every day.

When he was younger, he had visited a house where a party was going on, and some were playing with the occult. They were summoning spirits and trying to communicate with them; he was curious and participated a little bit. That night, when he got home, he had the experience of something sexual stimulating him. It felt completely real and physical, not some kind of fantasy, but he was alone. He made the mistake of giving in to the experience. Once he gave in that first time, the experience immediately turned to kinds of violation that had not stopped for almost a decade. The things he described to me wounded my heart to hear them, and I have never repeated them or written them down. In addition to the violations he endured, he would feel heavy weights pressing down on his body. When he would try to sleep, it was like bags of cement were piled on him and the bed would bend and his body would feel crushed, resulting in real damage to his spine over the years. He was agitated, sleep deprived, and tense. At the same time, he was lucid and clear in his thinking and speech.

I prayed with Brad one to three times a week for a year. I would pray the Litany of the Saints, as usual, and sometimes the Psalms or New Testament readings. During that year, he was delivered three times. Each time, it occurred randomly during prayer. He would suddenly relax and smile, and peace would spread across his face. But it would last for fifteen or twenty seconds, then the torment resumed. He was always incredibly grateful, however, even for those brief periods of relief. I was not completely sure about his case until I saw something very unusual for myself.

Brad was sitting in a rolling office chair, as was I, about six feet away and facing him. As I was praying, he moaned that the weights had just started crushing his foot anew. I was unsure what to do, so I addressed the (good) angels and just said, "Could you guys pull that off his foot?"

The next moment, I watched his leg get pulled up off the floor like someone was going to pull a boot off his foot, and then he was dragged across the room as if a strong force was pulling on his foot. I watched carefully, and he was not pushing himself across the floor with his other foot, nor was he touching anything with his hands. After being pulled about six feet, his foot dropped and he said the weights were gone.

After that year, life took me further away from the coast and I was no longer able to visit Brad. He updated me every few years since, usually if a new priest exorcist was willing to pray with him. He asked for prayers, hoping that he would finally be freed. Brad's case really drove home how pernicious the cases are that stem from sexual congress with demons. It is a hard thing to put in a book, but the potential lifelong horror that may be avoided is worth it.

Chapter 18

A Life Dissipated

Dr. James Benedict was a young man in the early 1970s. He was in medical school and had started his year of additional training to become a psychiatrist. He was very interested in helping people and finding effective and innovative ways to improve their lives. At the same time, California in the 1970s was open to many alternative ideas. It was then that a woman named Jane Roberts started channeling the speech of a spirit called Seth.

In the 1960s, Jane and her husband had paranormal manifestations going on in their home. Then she had an experience while sitting to write, as if she were receiving information from another source—not typical inspiration, but like something outside her was feeding her notions. She and her husband started using a Ouija board to investigate what was going on. It was through the board that something told them to call it Seth. After using the board for a while, Jane thought she could hear the spirit's voice directly in her mind. Then the trances started.

Jane would go into a trance, and she would speak in a deep voice with an odd accent. The voice claimed to be Seth. Her husband took notes of what this spirit said. Soon, they were charging people money to come and witness these channeling sessions, and some books were even written, compiled from material she dictated as Seth. These books led to fringe groups around the country that formed to study and to embody the spiritual teachings Jane gave in her trances, which included the idea that you create your own world through your thoughts and that you can get in touch with spirits to guide your life. These two promises are a powerful temptation, promising us powers and privileges that belong to God alone. The *New York Times* described Jane's message as a "guilt-free, me-first self-help program,"[13] and her success led to many similar mediums and channelers popping up around the country. By the later 1970s, there were many making money off similar books and appearances. Later, after Jane died in 1984, many channelers claimed to be in touch with Seth and tried to cash in on the fame she had built.

James read some of these books and was impressed by them, finding their teachings to ring true. There were many spiritualism groups near him in California, as well as groups that used physical divination devices, like the Ouija board, to communicate with spirits. One particular group caught his attention, and he made a trip to see them.

The group was open to and interested in having a psychiatrist-in-training visit them and witness their techniques. They were keeping long diaries of experiments and the dictated communications from the spirits through the board. The group was mature and very serious about the path they were on; they really thought they were getting in touch with the divine and were being guided by it. The group primarily used a Ouija board after a meditation session. Four members of the group used the board, and others

---

[13] Sam Kestenbaum, "Till Death Do Us Part," *New York Times*, October 29, 2019, https://www.nytimes.com/2019/10/29/style/seth-spirit.html.

recorded everything that was spelled out. They would rotate these roles, as some members were left just to watch at each session.

The dictated words that day addressed several things, including spelling out Dr. Benedict's full name, including his middle name, which he had not disclosed to the group. The apparent spirit spelled out that James had an important mission in this life and that he would have many breakthroughs and become an important and famous psychiatrist. It then mentioned details of an experience in his youth when he decided to become a doctor and how he felt that day. This impressed James; he could not see an explanation outside of a manifestation of the supernatural.

The next time he visited, he took part in meditation and a Ouija board session. The spirit seemed to tell him to practice the Ouija board three more times with the group, and so he did so over the rest of that summer in 1974. At the last visit, the board said that he now could use a Ouija board of his own, alone, back at school, but that he was to do so secretly. The special guidance and truths he would receive from it were for him alone, as he had been deemed special by the divine.

Over the rest of his medical training, he used the Ouija board alone. Initially, it was slow and awkward, but he found that with practice, it became easier. Dr. Benedict kept notes of what was said, then switched to audio recording so he could dictate the messages without pausing to write. He was promised divine favor, guidance, and insights that would help thousands. He was also encouraged to stay humble, as these favors would make him wealthy and busy in his professional life.

As his medical training was wrapping up, he suddenly got a new kind of message from the board. This time, instead of promising a generally successful future, it gave a specific instruction: he was to move to Chicago and take a position at a particular hospital there, where he was to seek collaborative work with a particular doctor. The board said that after this act of obedience, he would be rewarded. So Dr. Benedict contacted the hospital and applied for a position. He was offered a part-time job and the option to work additional hours at satellite clinics to fill out his week; the job provided just enough work to pay his medical school loan payments and to live in a decent apartment.

As his second year was starting in Chicago, the board said that he had a special mission: he was to move to Mexico City, where a position was said to be waiting for him serving the poor and those with substance abuse problems. He had only just started to establish himself in Chicago, and leaving before attaining a full-time position would hurt his resume. In the end, however, he obeyed the board and made the move, using most of his savings to pay the required six months up front on an apartment lease in Mexico.

What followed was decades of similar directives and moves, with the promised success always moving further down the road. He managed to work and pay off his medical school debts, and he did write some books on his ideas about treatment of psychosis. But, by the time he approached the Church for help, he was almost broke.

I met Dr. Benedict in the mid-2000s. He was at or past retirement age. He was only passing through my city on a temporary arrangement. The doctor never stayed in one place very long; in fact, he had been moving every few months for years at that point. He described finally, after these many years, doubting that the spirit talking to him through the Ouija board was acting in his best interests. But he was conflicted, after devoting his life to it, about making a change. Living at the whim of a Ouija board was all he seemed to know.

Meeting this sad doctor was a powerful thing. We sat on the porch of a house he was staying in and talked for hours. The fruits of the New Age are so different from its promises. Most people get nothing lasting out of it—just vague platitudes and affirmations that they are special. Some go a bit deeper and end up ruined. Dr. Benedict was not willing to renounce his spirit communication, and he was not open to being prayed over. I could rather easily detect some pride, even arrogance, about his clinical powers and judgment. Part of what he seemed to be struggling with was the act of really asking for help, which would include an admission that he had misjudged something—very badly.

I never heard from Dr. Benedict again. He had said he was continuing to head west and was not sure where he would be led after that. The commands had become a vague "head west" instead of specific cities and jobs. The spirit wasting his life had almost completed its work. How many more lives might he have touched if he had consistently worked as a doctor?

Chapter 19

Be Careful Whom You Sleep With

One morning at the diocese, my phone rang. The security woman who ran the front door said, "Adam, there is a woman. I put her in the conference room down here. She's one of yours."

Cindy had not called the diocese ahead of time, as most people do. A little confused, I went down to the conference room near the front entrance. A woman was sitting there alone. She acknowledged me, but she had a wide-eyed, upset, but also noticeably vacant look on her face. She started talking in a strained voice, and tears started flowing down her cheeks. Cindy did not seem to be aware of the tears, though, and she had not wiped them like we all do instinctively. She said, "This woman is possessed. We are in her because of _____, who has cursed her. We do not want to be in this woman, she prays too much. You have to help her."

Then she blinked and continued in a more emotional and human voice, "I'm sorry, that wasn't me. I need help. I don't know what's happening to me. I don't know why I came here today or how I got here."

I did an intake interview and asked her many questions. She had gotten into a relationship with a man who practices black magic. After she had sex with him, she started having bad nightmares and losing time. She suspected that he drugged her on other occasions, and she would wake up in different places. She then started losing whole days, or groups of days. One time, she came to in the street, having been badly beaten.

She said when she saw some of his books and paraphernalia, she realized he was into black magic. She immediately broke up with him and tried to keep him away from her, but he wouldn't leave her or her parents alone. Since then, the periods of lost time had continued—including that morning. We scheduled a prayer session to test for the signs of possession, and I asked her to get a psychological report from her therapist. She provided this, and she showed some of the signs of possession that we have discussed earlier.

The exorcisms were very dramatic in the beginning. Many spirits who claimed to be those worshiped in Santeria (a syncretic religion of the Caribbean), were cast out of the woman. Many bellowed and howled in husky male voices and bragged that they were still worshiped in the world as gods. In the end, however, they were all cast out. But then a different set of spirits started acting up. They insisted that they did not know by what right they were there and that Satan put them in the woman without any specific orders. Father ordered Satan to come and to answer the question. The demons protested and tried to dissuade us from doing so, which they always do. A few seconds later, the woman spoke in a very matter-of-fact way, "Fine, I'm here. What do you want?"

Father asked why he had his demons possessing this woman and by what right they were there. There was a pause and the voice continued in a business-like manner, as if reading a file, "Cindy Beeres, 47 years old. When she was four, I noticed that she had a strong mind and a gift from God of visualizing things of a spiritual nature. When she was six, I revealed myself to her in her room, and she could see me. I realized she had a vocation to the religious life, so I had to stop her from getting closer to God. I'm leaving."

Now the other demons were back again. The case has continued for a number of years, and many spirits have been cast out of Cindy. She has almost no impairment in life, and spirits no longer speak out of her, except during exorcism sessions. God willing, she will be completely freed soon.

Chapter 20

The Doctor's Mansion

Dr. Meres is a young Catholic physician who had recently transferred to Pittsburgh to take a position in one of the major trauma hospitals here. His wife, a Protestant, is also a physician. They bought a grand old home on ten acres of landscaped trees, gardens, and gazebos. The house was a bit run-down when they bought it, as were the grounds, but they intended to fix it up to their taste over time, while retaining the old-world charm of the estate.

The house was vacant when they looked at it, but it had been owned by another family for some time. There were still things here and there that needed to be cleared out before closing. Everything went smoothly, and when they took ownership, the house was empty—except for one item. In the large attic, there was a single old, framed print leaning against the rafters, literally the only thing left behind in the entire house. They wondered at it, since it was right in the middle of a well-lit area, easily seen from the doorway into the attic.

In the first few weeks, the family was busy unpacking, planning, having contractors in, or buying things for the home. After a couple of months, the place was mostly set up, and they settled into their new routine. They noticed some noises in the house, but they attributed them to the home being so old and large. Then one day, when Dr. Meres came home from his shift and put his bag on the kitchen island, it was swept off the surface by an unseen force and flew a few feet away, landing on the floor. He was alone in the kitchen. Then he heard a thump, similar to the noises they heard at night, in another part of the house. This pattern continued for several days. There were noises in the house only when he was home, and his keys or bag, or other small things, would be thrown across the room when he came home.

The doctor's wife, even though she was not Catholic, insisted that he call the diocese to ask for help. I talked with Dr. Meres, and we set up a visit for two days later. He did not seem too upset, but he also did not like his things being thrown around. One point that he made very strongly was that he knew a lot about the science of consciousness, since he was an anesthesiologist. He affirmed that he was completely awake and cogent when these events happened and that his wife had seen them with him. He said that he never gave any thought to ghosts or hauntings, but he knew that this was absolutely real and happening.

The couple told some of their friends about the apparently haunted mansion they had bought. Their friends came over the next night, before my visit, to see for themselves; they thought the idea of a haunted mansion was pretty cool. While they were having wine and talking about the house, the couple told their friends that they suspected that the old painting left in the attic was the cause of the haunting. They assumed the previous family had left it because it caused them problems as well. The friends were excited at the idea of a haunted painting and immediately offered to take it. The doctor and his wife happily gave it to them, feeling a good deal of relief to get rid of it.

We arrived the next evening and talked with the couple. Things had been quiet for the last twenty-four hours. Father did the house exorcism, house blessing, and Epiphany Blessing of the Threshold. Everything went smoothly and there was not a strong sense of a presence in the house. They thanked us, and we left.

The next morning, I got to the chancery at the usual time, about eight o'clock. I was up in my office for about ten minutes when my phone rang. Our security person at the front door said, "Some people just dropped off a big painting. They looked shaken up. They said it is ruining their lives and please take it. I'm assuming this is one of yours?"

I came down and brought the painting to my office. It was an old print behind glass. The picture was a simple, faded pastoral scene of a house in the country, and the frame was ornate but also dingy, dusty, and somewhat loose. It did not look like anything special to me. I saw a priest friend and asked them to quickly exorcise it just in case. After lunch that day, I examined the print again and pulled the thin wood backing away, revealing old, yellowed newspapers sandwiched between the print and the backing. I carefully pulled the papers out; they were brittle with age. Laying the pieces out on my desk, I was surprised to see that each piece had stories of murders on them, four in total, from different dates in the same year: 1943. I called Dr. Meres to confirm that this was the painting from their attic; it was.

Meanwhile, the house situation seems to be resolved, since we never heard back from Dr. Meres or his wife.

Chapter 21

Down on the Farm

The Bell family was my first case where law enforcement intersected with the spiritual. The Bells had moved to their small farm in a West Virginia valley about six years ago—one of those Appalachian valleys full of coal mines and tunnels. Initially, things were perfect, but it did seem, perhaps surprisingly, that they were one of very few Christians in the area. But then small, strange events started to happen. They would come home in the evening and find the attic light on, knowing for sure that they had left it off. They would hear pots and pans bumping and making noises in the kitchen in the middle of the night. Then they heard indecipherable voices talking in the basement when nobody was down there.

Then people—real, physical people—began to try to intimidate them. One day, they saw a car with five people wearing hoods sitting in their driveway, motionless and staring. Then a wheel on their car fell off while driving, and they discovered that all the lug nuts had been loosened. They found a lookout dug into their hill above their house with a bench and binoculars there.

Then the break-ins started. They would come home and find the front door open, but nothing in the house was disturbed or missing; in one instance, there was cash on the dining room table that was left untouched. After these break-ins, the manifestations in the house would seem to increase, and they would sometimes find odd objects hidden in the house. The husband had guns, and they changed the locks and set up a video security system. But somehow the video would turn off or go to static during the invasions. The local police then tried to set up their own surveillance equipment, but this also failed when intruders were about to enter the property and the police never found any leads. Meanwhile, the police told them that there had been so many calls for paranormal disturbances in the area that they had nicknamed it "Haunted Valley." In the end, the police gave up, as the equipment failures were uncanny and unexplainable.

On my first visit, it took over an hour for them to describe for me all they had been through. They were angry, but not afraid: they had strong faith, and the wife had considered the religious life in her youth and maintained a strong prayer life. I made monthly visits for nearly two years after break-ins and would pray, find the cursed object hidden in the house, bless the house and doorways, and leave. Then there would be another break-in, the chalk blessing on the threshold would be smeared, and the manifestations would start again.

Those years felt like a push and pull between whatever group was trying to drive the family away and the Church that was defending them spiritually. Eventually, the family stopped calling for assistance, and it seemed things had finally settled for them. It could have been related to their son and his fiancée moving back to the house, meaning that more adults were present more often.

I would later learn that occult groups often like caves and mines, as they are places with one entrance and exit where they can make noise without being heard. We never learned for sure what was happening in Haunted Valley, but it was far more than a haunting: there were people who wanted the Bells out, and they were willing to enlist spirits to help them succeed.

Chapter 22

Excalibur It Wasn't

Richard and his wife were devout Catholics and successful professionals with four children. Their house was a new construction, but there had been strange manifestations since shortly after moving in: small things would go missing and return; there would be phantom footsteps upstairs; there was a knocking sound in the attic but no person or animal was present; and a shadowy figure would appear at the other end of the upstairs hall but disappear as soon as someone got close. They had turned to a friend who claimed to be sensitive to spirits, but that only seemed to make things worse.

Then the family's thirteen-year-old son started to behave strangely. He was fine when he was away from the house, and perfectly normal at school, but had terrible nightmares and would sometimes go very quiet at home. He would silently sit still and stare blankly for hours. Then, Richard found his son standing and staring in one particular spot in the upstairs hallways over and over. The boy would slowly respond to his father, muttering that he was unsure what he had come upstairs for. At that point, the family called the diocese and asked for help.

An exorcist visited, talked with the family, and performed a house blessing and house exorcism. About a week later, Richard called to say that things went quiet for a few days, but then started to ramp back up.

I was called to consult on the case and performed a fresh intake interview with Richard. Everything about him seemed normal—and then we talked about his younger years. He had gotten pretty deeply involved in a martial art that focused on manipulation of "chi," or spiritual energy, in the body. Richard had done this martial art for a number of years, then his teacher started teaching him about manipulating and projecting "chi" through a sword. Richard meditated in special ways, practiced a lot with the sword, and studied books about "chi." After some time, he started to think he felt a tingling energy moving through his body when he meditated or practiced with the sword. By this time, he was finishing college and getting ready for graduate school, during which he stopped practicing this martial art.

Even though he had quit the meditation and other practices, I asked about the whereabouts of the sword. He said that he thought it was still in his things that he had packed away when moving to graduate school and, in fact, might be in the attic. He checked and found it stored in a bin directly above where his son would stand and stare blankly so many times. We removed the sword from the house, and Richard renounced any spirits he came into contact with through seeking those spiritual powers. After that, everything returned to normal for his son and the home.

Chapter 23

Reiki

Reiki is a pseudoscientific method of manipulating "energy" in a person by moving your hands near them with the intent to heal or otherwise affect this "energy." It was invented in Japan in the 1920s and came to the United States around 1970. It has been evaluated many times over the years, and rigorous study has found the practice has no effect beyond the power of suggestion.

As Reiki has become very popular in the United States, the United States Conference of Catholic Bishops Committee on Doctrine studied it thoroughly and released a document in 2009 called "Guidelines for Evaluating Reiki as an Alternative Therapy." They concluded that Reiki is incompatible with Christian spirituality, as it claimed a power to heal in humans that is not related to God, who is the source of all healing. They also cited the many studies that showed there is no demonstrable effect of Reiki on health.

> Since Reiki therapy is not compatible with either Christian teaching or scientific evidence, it would be inappropriate for Catholic institutions, such as Catholic health care facilities and retreat centers, or persons representing the

Church, such as Catholic chaplains, to promote or to provide support for Reiki therapy.[14]

The attraction of Reiki seems to be the same as all other New Age practices. First, it puts the person at the center of the spiritual system: you are the spiritual healer, not God. Second, it claims that one has special powers that need only to be awakened, feeding the ego and making one feel special. Finally, it offers heady promises without the burden of a moral system by which one is judged. Systems like this essentially borrow only the ego-friendly fantasies of eastern religions but leave their moral systems behind. To reiterate, everything about the New Age, including Reiki, essentially recapitulates the temptation in the Garden of Eden: with this secret knowledge, you can be like God!

Clair had gotten involved in Reiki twenty years before coming to the Church for help. She had good intentions and thought she was helping people and even moved on to promoting Reiki and teaching it herself. It became a part of how she made a living, and much of her identity was connected to the attention it caused people to give her.

Eventually, though, her fortunes changed. While she was promoting the practice, there was no reason for the demons to show their true nature to her. But at some point, they seem to have decided that she was no longer useful, and so they turned on her and started tormenting her, causing experiences of severe oppression and borderline possession when we prayed over her.

---

[14] "Bishops' New Guidelines Condemn Reiki Therapy as 'Superstition,'" Catholic News Agency, March 29, 2009, https://www.catholicnewsagency.com/news/15518/bishops-new-guidelines-condemn-reiki-therapy-as-superstition.

Her oppression symptoms were typical: repeating demonic nightmares, sleep deprivation, phantom scratches and bites, and strange manifestations in her house that made her scared to be at home. Spirits also spoke to her in her mind, addressing Reiki as well as telling her that God had abandoned her and no longer loved her. When we prayed over her, she would go into fits and hiss and sputter in a strange voice, sometimes striking out at the priest or those assisting. After many months of prayer, though, she experienced some small relief from her torment. Then she renounced Reiki and took down all of her social media posts about it. She went on to receive help in the Unbound deliverance system[15] that was being run by a reputable priest in her city, and as far as we know, she is doing well now.

There has been much confusion about Reiki because there are Catholic institutions that teach it and nuns and priests who promote it. It is clear, however, that the Church does not endorse Reiki or other New Age practices, and for good and thoughtful reasons. In the exorcism world, we have seen many cases that arise from Reiki, as well as yoga, particularly Kundalini Yoga.

Kundalini Yoga is a branch of yoga that focuses on the spiritual dimension of the practice. It works with the idea that every human being has the spirit of a serpent sleeping in the base of his or her spine, and it claims that through doing yoga one can awaken this spiritual serpent and allow it to slowly rise up the spine until it reaches the "crown chakra," or the top of the head. When this happens, the evidence is said to include involuntary spasms and

---

[15] This system of deliverance work is described in the book *Unbound*, by Neal Lozano. It is designed to address temptation and oppression cases, not possession. It focuses on repenting for sins and forgiving others, and then praying that spirits be driven away and stop bothering the person.

animalistic vocalizations. Some people also experience an inability to sleep, racing thoughts, strange sensations in the body, and so on. Many people report having their lives significantly disrupted for years after "awakening their Kundalini."

Finally, it is notable that the founder of Kundalini Yoga, Yogi Bhajan, has recently come under scrutiny after many of the women that were around him in the 1970s accused him of being a sexual predator.

Part IV

All Hell Breaks Loose

In which my work becomes a matter of life and death — my own

Chapter 24

Victories and Attempted Revenge

The exorcist community is still fairly small, both nationally and globally, so it is not unusual for friends to visit each other and to help with cases while in town. Most dioceses have several cases going at any time, and it can be good to get a fresh perspective from other experienced people. In one case, I visited a Texas diocese along with an additional exorcist friend, creating a weeklong team of three at that week's sessions.

There were multiple serious cases going on in the diocese, but one seemed to be the focus that week. Through the prayers of His Church, Jesus really humbled and cast out a number of major demons from this person that week. The demons railed that it was not fair that we were all together and that they should not all be subjected to being cast out in a single week. Toward the end of those sessions, we were dealing with a demon giving the same name as the one featured in the famous opening scene of the movie *The Exorcist*. This demon was an Assyrian/Babylonian spirit known for bringing famine and pestilence and is also associated with wind.

It was nothing like the movie, though. This demon is associated with filth and pestilence, and when I've encountered him, a miasma like rotting trash radiates from the person, but it disappears when the demon leaves or is cast out. In this case, he was particularly angry at me and kept leaning over with his eyes closed and hissing, "You should be more worried about yourself than this one. You should be more worried about yourself ..."

The sessions wrapped up for the week, and we flew to our respective homes. Two days later, I got a call from an old case in my home city from a man who had asked for help about four years previously.

We had tried to help him back then, but we were unsuccessful. Afterward, he called us and apologized, explaining that he had lied about the extent of his involvement with satanism and was not ready to give it up. He asked for help again two years later, but once again he held back some of the truth, and without his honesty and resolve, nothing could be done for him. Now he was back again.

He said that he was sorry that he had lied to us in the past but that this time was different. He said that the demons were going to kill him that night and that I had to come help him right away. I said firmly that I was not going to come to a bad part of town on a Friday afternoon when there was nobody to come with me, especially given his history of deceit. He started crying and sounded terrified of something. Then we were disconnected.

A few seconds later, the phone rang again. He was still crying and said, "I'm sorry. They told me they are very angry about the last two things you did to them. They told me I had to get you over here tonight and hurt you." His voice then changed to a strange, buzzing, confident voice. "You should be more worried about yourself. We're going to kill you. You should have left us alone in Texas." The voice then prattled on about a number of topics. I did not respond but was waiting to see if the man came back to his senses and really wanted to talk. After a few minutes, the voice said, "Yes, we are destroying the Church. But of course, He won't allow that, so we are just waiting to see what He does."

The voice then paused, as if considering what it had just said. It abruptly said, "Don't worry about this one, we'll make sure he gets a paycheck," and the phone was slammed down.

There are situations like this that start to cross over into real danger to life and other criminal activity. Demons are limited in what they can do, since they are under the authority of God. But people who choose to serve them can be genuinely dangerous.

Chapter 25

Covens, Cults, and SRA Cases

In the early 1990s, there were a number of cases of purported "satanic ritual abuse" (SRA) of children, in which many adults were charged with heinous crimes. Later, it was discovered that the events did not in fact take place, and many good people's reputations and lives were destroyed. In most cases, the children were complying with leading questions that dredged up false memories. This was often combined with poorly done hypnosis, which we also know can create false memories because people in a hypnotic trance are very vulnerable to even subtle suggestions.

It's hard to believe now, but at that time, there were many talk show episodes and sensational news stories about national networks of satanic groups that were running daycares, and so on. After some major lawsuits, and the overturning of several convictions, the pendulum began to swing the other way. The FBI eventually released a report that they found no evidence of the existence of satanic cults operating in the United States on an organized scale. The reality, in my experience, is somewhere in between: there are criminal satanic cults, but they aren't extremely organized and widespread.

For instance, during graduate school, I learned of a victim of satanic ritual abuse who was living in a police safe house while being treated psychologically for the trauma she had endured. Apparently, members of the group that she used to belong to were leaving strange messages on her therapist's phone, showing up at the clinic, and acting vaguely threatening in their efforts to find her. Things went over the line when a gun was fired blindly into the house of a professor overseeing the woman's treatment. She went on to list all the names and jobs of the people in the cult. This was sent with a cover letter to the cult from staff at the clinic, threatening to release the information if anyone was harmed or suddenly disappeared.

Around that same time, the false memory syndrome was being exposed in the courts, and an unusual document was given to all the graduate students in our psychology program to sign. The document had us affirm that recovered memories are not real and that we opposed the use of hypnosis to recover memories. The implication was that if we did not sign off on these statements, we would be dismissed from the program.

Over the years, I have worked with local, state, and federal law enforcement on various cases that involve crime related to black magic, exorcisms, covens, or cults. I have also assisted as an expert witness for two different public defenders on cases related to alleged possession. I am friends with some reporters and know that police sometimes scrub crime scenes or a suspect's residence of signs of black magic before allowing the press to see them. I know that law enforcement knows that these things go on, but there seems to be a desire to keep it out of the official story.

We have also had exorcism cases where cult members were trying to harm or to kidnap the people seeking help. Several times, we have had armed, uniformed police officers assist us with security while we met with victims of cults. Despite our efforts, violence has sometimes occurred, and, in one case, people have gone to federal prison. We have seen evidence that some members of these cults have roles of influence, such as one case where someone was victimized by them while medically vulnerable in a supposedly secure hospital.

In one case, an exorcist friend asked me to meet with him and a Pennsylvania Child and Youth Services (CYS) worker. The worker was a Catholic deacon who had come across something related to a cult: a woman was going to have an off-the-books baby for them, but she fled and went to the police. Her maternal instincts had kicked in, and she decided that she did not want her baby to die. These pregnancies, carried by women called "breeders" within these groups, are usually cared for by a doctor in the cult so that the pregnancy is never medically documented; therefore, the baby does not exist in any official records.

After this particular woman went to the police, they referred the case to CYS, who sent the deacon to investigate. This group owned about five houses in a cluster where their members lived. These members were mostly retired military who had been exposed to the cult while deployed overseas. I was later told that, in the end, the judge considered the entire situation to be a matter of "lifestyle choice," and so no action was taken. Needless to say, that seemed very suspicious to me.

So while I don't think there is an organized national network of satanists abducting thousands of children a year, I'm quite sure there are local groups that do actual harm.

As a side note, these criminal groups are superficially different from the satanist groups that seek public attention and political action, but that shouldn't reassure us too much. Those groups usually claim actually to not believe in, or to worship, Satan, but rather to be atheists or humanists who (for some reason) enjoy the trappings of satanism. These more visible groups usually aren't out there committing crimes (but of course they would deny it if they were). They do seem, however, to serve as a more palatable version of satanism for people who may be interested in exploring it. I suspect they are a kind of gateway drug to more serious and dangerous layers within the black magic community.

I hope it is clear to the reader that these types of cases are complex and involve many legal, moral, and ethical issues. I won't be sharing the details of any example cases because of this sensitivity and because it is impossible to do so without scandalizing or traumatizing the reader with the facts involved. Hopefully, the shallow bit I have shared has conveyed enough, without generating too much shock or upset.

Chapter 26

Satan Part 1: A Meeting in the Desert

An American diocese in the Southwest was establishing an exorcism ministry in 2008, and they came across a case they wanted help with. As I left the airport and drove into the desert for the first time, I was reminded of the Gospel stories that took place in such an environment.

I sat in on a few exorcisms for other cases, and then it was time for the difficult case. The afflicted had been quite violent, and so he wrapped a sheet around himself and lay down on the floor before the prayers started. As we prayed, the person blacked out, and the spirit took over his body. He got his hands free fairly quickly and started wrestling with the three of us, who were trying to gently control him. Oddly, he did not say anything. After a few minutes, I saw blood on the hands of the person's family member, who had been cut badly by fingernails. Then I realized something else strange: the spirit was not responding to any of the exorcist's questions or commands; it wasn't even saying "no!" or mocking us. Normally, the authority Jesus gave the apostles and is leant to the exorcist by his bishop compels the demons to answer the questions. Even if they resist for a while, they eventually provide some answer. Here, there was no obedience.

This was especially notable because part of the opening of each exorcism is a command not to harm anyone present. In the many dozens of exorcisms I had assisted with, I had never seen someone actually wounded. We might end up tired and sore, but the demons never actually hurt us. Something was wrong. That session ended, and the person and his family went home. The team discussed the blood, but I'm not sure they were as disturbed by the breaking of the rules as I was.

The next morning, I prayed in the chapel alone for a while, asking God what was going on with this case. In one of the few times this has happened, an answer seemed to pop into my mind: "Judas." I understood this to mean Judas Iscariot, the traitor to Jesus.

I told the exorcist my inspiration about Judas. I had never thought much about damned souls possibly being included in demonic possession. It wasn't unheard of in the literature, but the question was whether the demons were merely lying or perhaps taking on the names of famous people they had successfully influenced. There is also the warning in the *praenotanda*, or introductory instructions, of the old exorcism rite not to believe demons claiming to be damned souls.

Even so, many exorcists have encountered Judas, including in the case described in *Begone Satan: A Soul Stirring Account of Diabolical Possession in Iowa*, which has a *nihil obstat* and an *imprimatur*.[16] When damned souls seem to appear in solemn exorcisms, they are there as the property of the demons, not as the spirits running the possession. It is certainly possible that they are always demons pretending to be damned souls, but they do not have the powers

---

[16] Rev. Fr. Carl Vogl, *Begone, Satan: A Soul Stirring Account of Diabolical Possession in Iowa* (Rockford, IL: TAN Books, 1994).

of demons, and they are easily permanently removed from the case by asking St. Michael to return them to Hell, but I wouldn't know that until a bit later.

That evening, there was a planned session with the same person, and the same family members arrived and the same process was followed. Like last time, I saw cuts inflicted on the family members. The person seemed to be trying hard to gouge my hands and to cut me as well. When the exorcist's questions were going unanswered again, he tried, "Are you Judas?"

The person suddenly stopped wrestling and smiled. He looked at me and said, "Yes, I was sent here to scar you. So that for the rest of your life, you look and know that Hell has marked you."

The person then started fighting again, trying to gouge me with their nails. The exorcist ordered him to stop, but he did not obey. The session continued and eventually concluded; though the spirit seemed to try hard, whether it was a demon or Judas, it never cut me. After the session, we debated whether it could actually be Judas. No matter what, it was clear that it was an extremely unusual case.

The next day I was in the chapel alone again, this time asking, if it were actually Judas, how we should deal with him. Jesus gave authority to the Church over demons, not human souls. If it was Judas, it would make sense: he did not obey the order to do no harm, and he would not respond when ordered to answer questions. But how can you command him out if he ignores other orders? It seemed that it may work to ask an angel to take care of it, and what angel better than Michael? I passed on this idea to the exorcist, and he said he would try it during the next session. Unfortunately, it would be some time before I would find out if it worked.

That late afternoon, we had a session on a different case. This person did not have a history of violence like in the first case; he usually just sat in a chair during the exorcisms. The exorcist set the chair about six feet from the tabernacle, and as the exorcism started, it was more typical of what I had seen in the past. The only real wrestling came from the person trying to grab the exorcist's stole and pull it off. This is common because the purple stole is symbolic of his authority over the demons. I was able to gently open the person's grip and free the stole a number of times.

Then there came a strange moment. The exorcist abruptly stopped praying and looked at us. His assistant said, "I think Satan is at the back of the room."

We all seemed to have the same certain feeling that it was the case. The exorcist resumed praying, and the person grabbed his stole again. Two of us assistants looked at each other and whispered that it felt like Satan was getting closer, moving toward us. Then the possessed person went still for a moment. I was still trying to gently pull his grip loose from the stole when his fingers suddenly became like stone. I splashed holy water on the hand and all over the person. There was no reaction at all, not even a flinch. The person crossed his legs and leaned back in the chair in a haughty posture. Then he said, while looking at the tabernacle, "Why are you making me be here? You know how I hate these mortals."

The person paused and seemed to listen as if he were being spoken to, but we could hear nothing. Then he sighed and said, "Fine, but can I take one of them with me?"

The three of us looked at each other and raised our eyebrows. Apparently, the answer was no, thank God—literally. Then he turned his head slightly in my direction, without actually looking at me, and sneered, "You're no expert."

There was then a longer time in which the person seemed to be listening to something coming from the tabernacle. It seemed like Jesus was telling him something else, but we had no way of knowing. The spirit that may have been Satan then lowered his head and left the person's body. The demoniac was back to his normal human state, and the session ended.

That evening, we talked at length about both cases, and we tried to discern what God was trying to show us or teach us through these experiences. It would only be many years later that I understood a little more about Judas and Satan: it seems they usually travel together, since Satan was the one who tempted and possessed him in life.

Chapter 27

Satan Part 2: A Personal Grudge

In a sense, this next case was a culmination of fifteen years of work. Over the years, I had met many demons through the ministry of exorcism. Early on, it seems like it was mostly low-level spirits: since the angels fell from all nine choirs, there are likely nine ranks of spirits among the demons as well. In more recent years, I had been present at exorcisms of just about all the major demons one finds in the Bible or hears about today. Then I had encountered demons who claimed to be the spirits currently, or historically, worshiped in various belief systems from around the world. And I had met Satan briefly a number of years ago, when he told me, "You're no expert."

We had recently worked on a case of a person who had been possessed for a long time; we weren't sure exactly how long. The person had gotten into trouble mainly through extensive use of the Ouija board and then through obsession with astrology. Once the demons got in, the person was unable to attend Mass; at best, he could only stand outside and listen. Meanwhile, he worked in the parish and helped teach children about the Faith. This went on for more than twenty years.

The person's parish priest felt moved to offer to meet and to pray with him. During those prayers, the person got severe headaches, sometimes swooned and passed out, and always felt terrible for hours afterward. The priest called me for advice, and since it seemed like simple oppression, I advised to just keep praying for the person and to see if things got better. About a month later, I got another call: the person had coughed up small nails during the prayer. At that point, we took the case over.

At the first meeting, we met in the rectory and talked with the person, but as we pressed further into his background, he seemed dizzy and distressed. Suddenly he coughed, and there were three or four shiny bits of metal on the tablecloth in front of him. He did not see them, but we did. As we talked a bit more, he coughed up several more pieces of metal: some looked like straightened staples, while others were typical nails you would use to hang a small picture. We moved into the church so we could start praying for him formally. He became unconscious and hit the floor hard as soon as he stepped across the threshold into the church. I had seen this before in severe cases.

For the next ten weeks, we performed some of the most challenging exorcisms I had ever been a part of. Sessions went for three, four, or even six hours. Many demons, including all of the major ones I had encountered over my career, and some I had never heard of anyone encountering, were cast out. They fought hard, and the general sentiment they conveyed was that this person was too important, and that if they lost him, their kingdom in the world would be shaken.

The demons mentioned that people who "were theirs" were coming. Members of a fairly well-known satanic cult (not a tame political group, but a dangerous criminal group that started in the 1960s) from another state began causing trouble, including a kidnapping that resulted in an arrest and time in a federal prison.

Police were present at some of the sessions to protect everyone involved in the exorcisms, and they helped us in other ways.

Meanwhile, Jesus seemed to be moving this case along very quickly. On some days, eight or more major spirits were cast out, as well as many minor ones. After about ten weeks, the person started being delivered spontaneously of the smaller demons. He would be with someone from the team, and suddenly the minor demons would manifest and scream as Jesus cast them out. The person said that it felt like they were rats escaping a sinking ship. He could tell that the demons were scared and wanted out because they knew they were losing.

Then the person said he overheard Satan talking with some of the demons. He said that Satan had requested—presumably of Jesus, as Satan and his demons can do nothing without permission from God—a personal confrontation with me. The person said that Satan hates me very much and wanted to kill me personally.

During the downtime between sessions, I would usually be at work at our chancery, and I would get texts or calls from the person saying that they were feeling odd and could use a prayer. I would pause and pray a Rosary or other prayers, asking God to help the person remain in control. Then I would sometimes get mocking texts from the demons manifesting in the person. One time, after praying a number of Rosaries, I got a text that read, "Fine, we are leaving him alone for now. It's because we choose to, not because of that woman you worship." Another time, I got a text in Greek. I forwarded a screen capture to someone who could get a quick translation: "I say again, I will not be moved. ____ you!" The possessed individual, I should say, did not know Greek, and that particular profanity isn't in online Greek dictionaries.

Up until Satan's arrival, the other major spirits had always complained, "Our kingdom will suffer if we lose this one," and

"They will do too much damage to us for Jesus," and so on, always in the first-person plural. When the last of the demons was cast out, however, there was a sudden and incredible burst of strength. I weigh about 220 pounds, and this person weighed significantly less than that, but he immediately overpowered me, even after his body had exerted itself for hours. One of the first things this new spirit said was, "I won't let you harm my kingdom!"

The next four days were spent in exorcisms against Satan. We were confident it was actually him for a few reasons. First, he did not react to sacramentals such as holy water, blessed salt, or relics. Second, his strength was much greater than what we usually see in exorcisms. Finally, he did not seem to care that an exorcism was going on. Once he manifested in the person's body, he just physically attacked me for hours.

But when commanded to say the date and time of his departure, he answered: in four days, at 3:00 p.m.

Meanwhile, the person repeatedly spit nails at icons or at the priest who was performing the exorcism. He would spit them about three or four feet, and accurately, mainly at images of St. Michael. By the end of a session, I would gather up ten or twenty nails (and, yes, we checked the person for nails he might've smuggled in or stashed in his mouth).

During the sessions, the person would grab me and whisper temptations in my ear: "Just give up. What do you want? I can get you whatever you want in this world"; "Don't take him to His kingdom; join me in my kingdom"; "Jesus picked the wrong people to try and save him; you're too weak; you can't do it." I would say "never" or "no" or just pray to Jesus that I trusted Him, and so forth. Then the violence would resume.

Sometimes he addressed one of the priests, but for some reason, he seemed to be mainly motivated by a personal hatred for me. It seems that Jesus allowed him to test me physically, and, more importantly, to tempt me. With the help of God, I had the physical strength to keep going, even when I was the only person restraining him for hours. The temptations, on the other hand, were easy to refuse since God is God, and that's that.

We got to the appointed day, and just before three o'clock we started the prayers for that day. I was holding the person and praying the Hail Mary near his ear. Satan was struggling, but then I heard the person's human voice whisper, "Keep praying that, keep praying!" Then I heard him say, "She's so beautiful, she's so beautiful!"

There was a strong shudder that went through the person's body, like a single huge convulsion. Then he went limp and unconscious. We gently held him up and waited. After about thirty seconds, his eyes fluttered open and stared for a moment as if lost in thought. He suddenly started laughing and sobbing with joy, and tears started rolling down his face. He simply said, "He's gone." It is often the case that Mary is sent by Jesus to announce the end of cases to the possessed person; it's something we have seen many times, and it is always incredibly moving to hear the person's love and awe at her visible presence and at the authority Jesus has given her. She is the woman who crushes the head of the serpent in the Book of Revelation.

Later, the person explained what he had experienced during the final session. He had partly come to his senses while we were praying and saw a woman in the church he had never seen before. He thought this woman had come to pray like the others—as always, we had a number of women there to pray in support—but then he realized that she was approaching from above, from the direction of an ancient icon of Mary that was in the church. He knew it was Mary, the Mother of Jesus, and she was indescribably beautiful. Mary looked at him and smiled, then turned to Satan and frowned. And all she said was, "It's over," and in a split second, the person felt like a hand reached in and pulled half of him out of himself. He suddenly knew with absolute clarity that it was over.

We set up for Mass and celebrated a Mass of thanksgiving. And he received Communion for the first time in over twenty years.

The person has gone on to attend Mass daily and to go to Confession regularly. There have been demonic attempts to tempt him in various ways, but Jesus has kept him safe. It seems that St. Michael is personally protecting him on his journey with God.

Why was Satan so intent on fighting me personally and trying to tempt me away from my work? I suppose it is because I have been involved in teaching priests about exorcism for fifteen years. I have written a pastoral manual for priests on exorcism—it is used in many places—and books to teach the public about the tricks and lies the fallen angels use to get into people's lives. It's not that I'm particularly special or holy (in fact I know that I am far from holy, a great sinner in fact); it is just that Jesus is using me to help bring the exorcism ministry back into a troubled world. I think Satan and his fallen angels do not like it, but that's too bad. There is only one God, and Satan has already been defeated.

Conclusion

These are only a sampling of the hundreds of cases I have worked on over the last fifteen years. My goal in sharing them is to encourage you to move toward God in prayer and in the focus of your daily life—and to show you what to avoid in order to stay safe and healthy, in both body and soul. God's rules are not there to ruin your life, but to spare you the troubles that follow from sin, including these entanglements with the evil spirits that come from First Commandment violations.

There are so many temptations to dabbling in spiritualism and the occult in our world today. They are all based on the lie that you can be like a god, if only you discover and harness the secret powers in yourself. This is the lie of Satan from the Garden of Eden, the New Age, Reiki, Kundalini Yoga, and black magic. The promise that you can force your will onto the world and other people through these forces is a trick: evil spirits do not and will never serve you; seeking powers from them only gives them permission to dominate you.

This is why consulting spirits with a Ouija board, by other physical means, or with a medium—even if you don't take it "seriously"—is incredibly dangerous. Only demonic spirits will respond, and eventually they will talk in your mind, then push you to suicide or possession. They want nothing more than to destroy you by destroying your faith in and relationship with God. The same goes for ghost hunting. Calling up the dead to talk with them, called necromancy in the Bible, is strongly forbidden by God and only leads to trouble later.

In order to strengthen yourself against the temptations and assaults of the demonic, I urge you to learn more about God and to seek Him directly through His Church. Participate in the Sacraments: the best defenses against the demons are prayer, avoiding all violations of the First Commandment, and a healthy and active sacramental life.

If you are not yet Christian, I urge you to learn more about Jesus. Instead of listening to the opinions of others, read what Jesus said and did for yourself. Read the Gospels of Matthew, Mark, Luke, and John. All the apostles, except John, who died of natural causes, died rather than renounce that they had seen Jesus risen from the dead. Would you die for a lie?

As we said in the beginning, our society no longer teaches these rules, but often celebrates breaking them. The problem with that is simply this: God is real, and the rules have not changed. Evil spirits work personally to tempt us into sin and collectively to normalize sin in society. Their goal is to coax us away from God and into a subservient relationship with them. They play nice in the beginning, but when they have a hold on us, they turn cruel and controlling. They strive to isolate us and drive us to despair—or sometimes possession.

In accord with Jesus' example and command, the Church has always prayed for deliverance for people and performed exorcisms. Sadly, and dangerously, this fell out of fashion for a while in the United States, but we have seen a great movement of the Holy

Spirit in this generation. We went from a handful of exorcists in this country fifteen years ago to hundreds today. We teach more in seminary, and we provide training as continuing education for priests. We are also, through books like these, pulling back the curtain on the supernatural. We are exposing how demons ensnare people and sharing the consequences of going down these dark roads.

But as the darkness has become more open and brazen, God has only revealed more of the love and freedom that comes from Jesus Christ—His only begotten Son, whom He sent into the world to pay for our sins and to open the way back to the Father for us.

Jesus loves you so very much.

Litany of the Saints

V. Lord, have mercy on us.

R. *Christ, have mercy on us.*

V. Lord, have mercy on us.

V. Christ, hear us.

R. *Christ, graciously hear us.*

V. God the Father of Heaven,

R. *Have mercy on us.*

V. God the Son, Redeemer of the world,

R. *Have mercy on us.*

V. God the Holy Spirit,

R. *Have mercy on us.*

V. Holy Trinity, one God,

R. *Have mercy on us.*

V. Holy Mary,

R. *Pray for us.* (Repeat after each invocation.)*

V. Holy Mother of God,

V. Holy Virgin of virgins,

V. Saint Michael,

V. Saint Gabriel,

V. Saint Raphael,
V. All ye holy Angels and Archangels,
V. All ye holy orders of blessed Spirits,
V. Saint John the Baptist,
V. Saint Joseph,
V. All ye holy Patriarchs and Prophets,
V. Saint Peter,
V. Saint Paul,
V. Saint Andrew,
V. Saint James,
V. Saint John,
V. Saint Thomas,
V. Saint James,
V. Saint Philip,
V. Saint Bartholomew,
V. Saint Matthew,
V. Saint Simon,
V. Saint Thaddeus,
V. Saint Matthias,
V. Saint Barnabas,
V. Saint Luke,
V. Saint Mark,
V. All ye holy Apostles and Evangelists,
V. All ye holy Disciples of the Lord,
V. All ye Holy Innocents,
V. Saint Stephen,
V. Saint Lawrence,
V. Saint Vincent,
V. Saints Fabian and Sebastian,
V. Saints John and Paul,
V. Saints Cosmas and Damian,

V. Saints Gervase and Protase,

V. All ye holy martyrs,

V. Saint Sylvester,

V. Saint Gregory,

V. Saint Ambrose,

V. Saint Augustine,

V. Saint Jerome,

V. Saint Martin,

V. Saint Nicholas,

V. All ye holy bishops and confessors,

V. All ye holy Doctors,

V. Saint Anthony,

V. Saint Benedict,

V. Saint Bernard,

V. Saint Dominic,

V. Saint Francis,

V. All ye holy priests and Levites,

V. All ye holy monks and hermits,

V. Saint Mary Magdalen,

V. Saint Agatha,

V. Saint Lucy,

V. Saint Agnes,

V. Saint Cecilia,

V. Saint Catherine,

V. Saint Anastasia,

V. All ye holy virgins and widows,

V. All ye Holy Saints of God,
R. *Make intercession for us.*

V. Be merciful,
R. *Spare us, O Lord.*

V. Be merciful,

R. *Graciously hear us, O Lord.*

V. From all evil,

R. *O Lord, deliver us.**

V. From all sin,

V. From thy wrath,

V. From sudden and unprovided death,

V. From the snares of the devil,

V. From anger, and hatred, and every evil will,

V. From the spirit of fornication,

V. From lightning and tempest,

V. From the scourge of earthquakes,

V. From plague, famine, and war,

V. From everlasting death,

V. Through the mystery of thy holy Incarnation,

V. Through thy coming,

V. Through thy Nativity,

V. Through thy baptism and holy fasting,

V. Through thy Cross and Passion,

V. Through thy death and burial,

V. Through thy holy Resurrection,

V. Through thine admirable Ascension,

V. Through the coming of the Holy Spirit, the Paraclete,

V. In the day of judgment,

R. *We sinners, beseech thee, hear us.**

V. That thou wouldst spare us,

V. That thou wouldst pardon us,

V. That thou wouldst bring us to true penance,

V. That thou wouldst vouchsafe to preserve our Apostolic
   Prelate and all orders of the Church in holy religion,

V. That thou wouldst vouchsafe to humble the enemies of holy Church,

V. That thou wouldst vouchsafe to give peace and true concord to Christian kings and princes,

V. That thou wouldst vouchsafe to grant peace and unity to the whole Christian world,

V. That thou wouldst restore to the unity of the Church all who have strayed from the truth, and lead all unbelievers to the light of the Gospel,

V. That thou wouldst vouchsafe to confirm and preserve us in thy holy service,

V. That thou wouldst lift up our minds to heavenly desires,

V. That thou wouldst render eternal blessings to all our benefactors,

V. That thou wouldst deliver our souls and the souls of our brethren, relatives, and benefactors from eternal damnation,

V. That thou wouldst vouchsafe to give and preserve the fruits of the earth,

V. That thou wouldst vouchsafe to grant eternal rest to all the faithful departed,

V. That thou wouldst vouchsafe graciously to hear us,

V. Son of God,

V. Lamb of God, Who takest away the sins of the world,
R. *Hear us, O Lord.*

V. Lamb of God, Who takest away the sins of the world,
R. *Graciously hear us, O Lord.*

V. Lamb of God, Who takest away the sins of the world,
R. *Have mercy on us.*

V. Christ, hear us,

R. *Christ, graciously hear us.*
V. Lord, have mercy on us,
R. *Christ, have mercy on us.*
V. Lord, have mercy on us.

Appendix II

Minor Exorcism

Laypeople: Do not say the Minor Exorcism.

The original exorcism prayer was long and only intended for priests to say. It was primarily directed toward the problem of Freemasonry, which was trying to destroy the Church. Over the years, the prayer was changed slightly, and eventually the St. Michael prayer was derived from it. The St. Michael prayer can be said by anyone and had been said after every Mass in the world for decades. Blessedly, it is making a comeback.

The revised form of the original exorcism prayer was placed in the Roman Ritual after the solemn exorcism. The rule, or rubric, for the prayer reads, "The following exorcism can be used by bishops, as well as by priests who have permission from their ordinary." This rubric has never been abrogated—though in some cases, it has been erroneously removed by those reproducing the prayer in print or on the internet, but the rule is still in force.

The problem with laypeople saying the minor exorcism is twofold. First, it is an act of disobedience, as they are not priests with permission from their bishop. Second, the prayer includes a direct command: "Begone, Satan!" This is a personal challenge between the priest and the demon that the priest issues with the apostolic authority of his bishop behind him. If a layperson gives this command, he or she only has himself or herself behind it. This can initiate a battle that a layperson has neither the authority, experience, nor the power to successfully complete.

One particularly difficult possession case arose in just such a way. Robert was a Catholic who was very involved in his parish. He had a Protestant minister friend who had been praying deliverance prayers for a member of his church without success. Robert told the minister about the minor exorcism and found a copy of it. They arranged for Robert to meet with the struggling woman and the minister at their church. He knew about the rule of the minor exorcism, but he decided to use it anyway. As he said the words of direct command, while touching her shoulder, he felt something rush into him through his arm. That night, he experienced full possession.

There is something very important about touch along with prayer, particularly when issuing commands, called *imprecatory prayer*. You really should only allow priests to touch you during prayer, as their hands are consecrated. If a layperson puts hands on someone and gives direct commands to a demon, they have consented to that demon pushing back. Likewise, if you consent to a layperson laying hands on you and praying, you are submitting to their personal spiritual authority and accepting whatever spiritual baggage they have. When you ask a priest to do the same, you are not accepting their personal spiritual baggage because they are acting in *persona Christi* and not as a particular human person.

There is a partial exception to this warning: in specific circumstances, where a Christian has full authority, he can command a demon to leave in the name of Jesus. These include the authority one has over one's own body and over the bodies of your children before the age of reason (seven years, in most cases). The father of a household also has authority over his home, but experience shows that it is best to ask the diocese to send a priest to do a house exorcism. I am not saying the father of the household could ever use the minor exorcism over his house; he cannot. Even in these cases, commands by laypeople should be done on an emergency basis, not a habitual one. If there is a lingering problem, you should work with your diocese to evaluate it and to provide the appropriate prayer.

About the Author

Adam Blai has been drawn into an interesting journey in spite of his sins. He first spent about fifteen years learning about the brain, mental illness, and forensic psychology. He then spent more than fifteen years assisting the exorcism ministry in the United States and elsewhere. He is a peritus (expert) on religious demonology and exorcism for his diocese and has taught priests and seminarians across the country. After being at hundreds of solemn exorcisms and working on thousands of demonic cases in some way, he has learned the ways people get into trouble. Now part of his work is informing the public about these things so they can choose whether to avoid them. In addition to seeing spiritual evil, he has seen spiritual good in the form of miracles and other extraordinary graces.

Sophia Institute

Sophia Institute is a nonprofit institution that seeks to nurture the spiritual, moral, and cultural life of souls and to spread the gospel of Christ in conformity with the authentic teachings of the Roman Catholic Church.

Sophia Institute Press fulfills this mission by offering translations, reprints, and new publications that afford readers a rich source of the enduring wisdom of mankind.

Sophia Institute also operates the popular online resource CatholicExchange.com. *Catholic Exchange* provides world news from a Catholic perspective as well as daily devotionals and articles that will help readers to grow in holiness and live a life consistent with the teachings of the Church.

In 2013, Sophia Institute launched Sophia Institute for Teachers to renew and rebuild Catholic culture through service to Catholic education. With the goal of nurturing the spiritual, moral, and cultural life of souls, and an abiding respect for the role and work of teachers, we strive to provide materials and programs that are at once enlightening to the mind and ennobling to the heart; faithful and complete, as well as useful and practical.

Sophia Institute gratefully recognizes the Solidarity Association for preserving and encouraging the growth of our apostolate over the course of many years. Without their generous and timely support, this book would not be in your hands.

www.SophiaInstitute.com
www.CatholicExchange.com
www.SophiaInstituteforTeachers.org

Sophia Institute Press is a registered trademark of Sophia Institute. Sophia Institute is a tax-exempt institution as defined by the Internal Revenue Code, Section 501(c)(3). Tax ID 22-2548708.